■ SCHOLASTIC

READ – ALOUDS
WITH HEART

Literacy Lessons That Build Community, Comprehension, and Cultural Competency

DANA CLARK, KEISHA SMITH-CARRINGTON, AND JIGISHA VYAS

SVP and Publisher: Tara Welty
Editor: Maria L. Chang
Cover design: Cynthia Ng
Interior design: Michelle H. Kim
Cover illustration: Shutterstock Inc.
Photos: Courtesy of the authors
Icons: Noun Project

ISBN: 978-1-338-86190-7
Scholastic Inc., 557 Broadway, New York, NY 10012
Copyright © 2023 by Dana Clark, Keisha Smith-Carrington, and Jigisha Vyas
Published by Scholastic Inc. All rights reserved.
Printed in the U.S.A.
First printing, March 2023.
1 2 3 4 5 6 7 8 9 10   40   30 29 28 27 26 25 24 23

TABLE OF CONTENTS

Dear Reader,

The book you now hold in your hands started as a seed of hope and a conversation between Dana (a White, cisgender woman), Jigisha (a Southeast Indian, cisgender woman), and Keisha (a Black, cisgender woman). Little by little, that seed was nurtured as the three of us brought together our dream of classrooms in which every child feels seen, valued, and loved. Together, we imagined spaces where learning centers multiple perspectives and celebrates collective knowledge, rather than competition. We imagined a space that would allow children to succeed as learners because their emotional needs were met first. We imagined interdependent communities working to ensure the holistic success of each member so the whole could thrive. We hoped, we came together, we envisioned, we imagined . . . and we studied. Our seed of hope grew as we began to formulate ways to co-create environments and learn with children in a classroom, resources to use, and lessons to teach. That became this book, which lays out our pathway to the classrooms we've been dreaming of.

On the surface, it may seem like this book is about mentor texts, but the reality is that it is way more than that. It is about creating a classroom community that centers students: honoring the identities of everyone in the room, undertaking thoughtful and empathetic reading, and engaging in action that strengthens the humanity of each member. We understand that you may be tempted to jump straight to the mentor texts and lessons. But in order to prepare to bring the beautiful books and lessons we describe into your work with children, you must first do work with yourself. We have learned that conversations around identity require that we study not only learning structures that will support children's social and emotional learning but also how our identities impact our ways of being with students.

It is our intention that the first part of this book act as both a guide and a journal so that you can dream up your own vision of the classroom you hope to create and get clarity on where your own identity journey begins. To that end, this foundational part has two distinct purposes. The Learning About Ourselves section is designed to act as a mirror—opening the door to reflective activities that invite you to analyze the ways you look at and respond to yourself and others who are and are not like you. In subsequent sections, activities and topics designed to help you bring a reflective stance to that reading are tagged with a little journal icon. The Learning About Our Practices section offers windows into possible practices that support community and literacy learning. This includes reading lenses and ideas on strategy instruction, tips on using circle practices to support learning, and ways to coach your readers as they transfer their learning into their own choice reading.

The Lessons Part of this book is designed as a menu. Choose a book. Choose a strategy. Choose a standard. Create your own adventure. While we do offer some possibilities on how to make these choices, there isn't a right or wrong way to bring the stories and lesson work into your classroom community. Our hope is that you can find the learning, books, and conversations that speak to you and help guide the next steps you take with your learners.

The Final Part speaks to ways you can move beyond our book recommendations to transfer our lenses and ideas to self-selected titles. Here, you will also find a personalized note from each of us.

Oh, and one last thing before you really dig in. One main tenet of this work is our belief in community. That belief extends beyond our classrooms. We believe that teaching and professional learning is also best done in community. While the beginning sections include reflection pages that will allow you to sit with yourself to reflect and imagine, we hope that you won't have to do this alone. We suggest you find a thinking partner who can support you through this first section. However, if you are on your own, please be sure to lean into some of the accompanying resources—and know that we are here with you, too.

Yours in learning and community,
Dana, Keisha, and Jigisha

Bonus online materials: To access additional mini-lessons and other resources, go to **www.scholastic.com/readaloudswithheart** and enter this password: **SC747201**.

THE LEARNING PART

Decades ago, in her powerful essay "Mirrors, Windows, and Sliding Glass Doors," Rudine Sims Bishop shared the importance of building classroom libraries in which all children can see themselves and their families in the pages of a book. She wrote: "When children cannot find themselves reflected in the books they read, or the images they see are distorted, negative, or laughable, they learn a powerful lesson on how they are devalued in the society of which they are a part" (1990). Every child deserves to feel acknowledged and valued in our classrooms. And yet more than 30 years after Bishop wrote those words, the representation of all children in our libraries and mentor texts is still lacking.

Since 1985, the Cooperative Children's Book Center (CCBC) has documented the number of books by and about Black people. In 1994, they added books by and about Indigenous and other People of Color to their statistics. In 2018, the CCBC also began collecting statistics for additional identities, such as LGBT+, disability, and religion. As the Diversity in Children's Books 2018 graphic below shows, we cannot depend upon the publishing industry to ensure that the faces our students see as they turn the pages of a book will match their own faces or those of the children sitting around them.

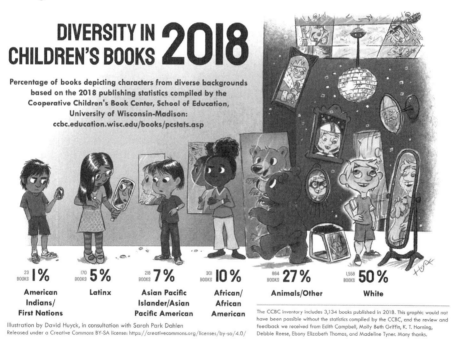

DIVERSITY IN CHILDREN'S BOOKS 2018

Percentage of books depicting characters from diverse backgrounds based on the 2018 publishing statistics compiled by the Cooperative Children's Book Center, School of Education, University of Wisconsin-Madison: ccbc.education.wisc.edu/books/pcstats.asp

23 BOOKS **1%**	170 BOOKS **5%**	218 BOOKS **7%**	301 BOOKS **10%**	864 BOOKS **27%**	1,558 BOOKS **50%**
American Indians/ First Nations	**Latinx**	**Asian Pacific Islander/Asian Pacific American**	**African/ African American**	**Animals/Other**	**White**

Illustration by David Huyck, in consultation with Sarah Park Dahlen
Released under a Creative Commons BY-SA license: https://creativecommons.org/licenses/by-sa/4.0/

The CCBC inventory includes 3,134 books published in 2018. This graphic would not have been possible without the statistics compiled by the CCBC, and the review and feedback we received from Edith Campbell, Molly Beth Griffin, K. T. Horning, Debbie Reese, Ebony Elizabeth Thomas, and Madeline Tyner. Many thanks.

While efforts over the past few years have increased representation across Black, Indigenous, and other People of Color (BIPOC), these groups are still woefully underrepresented in children's books. The responsibility to make sure that our classroom libraries and mentor texts provide children with window, mirror, and sliding glass door experiences falls on us as educators. Truly, there is no reason for our school libraries or classroom libraries to look like the image above. For this reason, Keisha works tirelessly with teachers, school librarians, and achievement coaches to create diverse collections in all the elementary and middle school spaces in her district. She also helps educators develop and strengthen the skills, knowledge, and dispositions they need to facilitate their and their students' cultural competence through literacy, inclusive not only of the strands of reading, writing, speaking, listening, and language, but also of critical literacy, gender literacy, and racial literacy.

We cannot stop at simply putting "diverse books" on our library shelves. First, as Chad Everett, chief instructional officer at Imaginelit.com, clearly explained in a blog post, "There is no diverse book" (2017). Using "[the] word *diverse* as it is currently used centers heteronormative whiteness as the default . . . labeling any single text as diverse stands in direct contradiction to the intended purpose of the call for diverse texts. A binary lens of diversity only further *others* the narratives of individuals from minoritized groups." This argument can be used to support the years of research by the CCBC, which has included and expanded the number of backgrounds, both minoritized and normalized, in its quantifications of diversity in publishing.

Second, it is not sufficient for the books to simply occupy space in rooms with children who may neither select nor have the capacity to fully comprehend stories that provide windows and sliding glass doors (Bishop, 1990). Children deserve expansive conversations about how identities shape the ways we read books and see the world. We who teach reading are familiar with the work of Louise Rosenblatt, whose transactional theory details the way a reader's identity shapes comprehension of a text (1986). This transaction, in which the reader brings the self while examining a text, is the point at which the text may be labeled as diverse for that individual reader (Rosenblatt, 2017).

Through deep and purposeful experiences with texts, children can learn and practice ways to explore their identity and build empathy for people with different identities. By intentionally curating collections that represent many group identities for both mini-lessons and choice reading, teachers provide children with opportunities to strengthen self- and social awareness and to engage in deep thinking and discourse that can increase competency in self-management, relationship skills, and responsible decision-making. These five competencies of social-emotional learning (SEL) "enhance" English language arts/literacy curricula (CASEL, 2017a). They also dovetail with the social justice standards (see page 18).

Anchoring Our Practice: Books Are the Key

In The Lessons Part of this book (starting on page 61), you will find thoughtfully chosen mentor texts that bring young readers stories of celebration, hardship, love, and loss. We have chosen to center a few of our favorite texts within this resource because we know that books can spark conversations that need to be had in our classrooms—conversations that may be uncomfortable or that we've been afraid to have because we aren't sure how to start them. Books allow us to lean on the words and pictures of authors and illustrators and invite children into thinking together.

Books are key to this work. We also know that as wonderful as interactive read-alouds can be, books alone are not the answer. We have found that teachers sometimes neglect the follow-up small-peer group work and individual work with texts that truly cement learning. So, along with the mentor text suggestions and information about the books themselves, we provide mini-lessons that offer a choice of strategies, circle questions, and carryover coaching prompts for independence that will bring important conversations to life in the classroom.

The strategies and prompts laid out in the book use three "reading lenses" to deepen children's understanding of texts and people: Identity, Harm and Healing, and Heartwork. Through these lenses, children sharpen reading comprehension skills, such as analyzing character, determining themes, and exploring perspectives. They also find their way to apply new understandings to their everyday interactions with one another.

Table 1: Reading Lenses

Identity 	Harm & Healing 	Heartwork ♥
The Identity work invites children to see characters as complex people who have layers—some chosen and some they were born with. These layers of identity blend together in each person to create a uniqueness of humanity. **We study:** • how the identities of characters are revealed. • how identity connects to motivation, needs, desires, and actions. • how reading through our own identities and experiences influences our thinking and connections to characters.	Inspired by restorative practices, the work of this lens focuses on studying problems, resolutions, and themes. Stories, both real and imagined, often center people's struggles and the pathways they find to healing—pathways that can teach us all a lot about life. **We study:** • how to identify internal and external struggles. • how to bring different perspectives to the problems in the text. • how struggles impact and motivate characters. • how to extract life lessons through the characters' responses to challenges.	The lens of Heartwork explores how readers can connect to the emotions of the characters and allow the stories to touch their hearts by noticing details and sharing perspectives. **We study:** • how to take on the perspective of the characters. • how exploring different perspectives helps us gather more complex understandings of characters. • how word choice and images help readers identify mood and tone. • how empathy can help us live differently.

Why Identity?

Before answering "why identity?", let's first explore this question: What is identity? Author and literacy leader Gholdy Muhammad defines identify as: "notions of who we are, who others say we are (in both positive and negative ways), and whom we desire to be" (Muhammad, 2020). Author and professor Janet Sauer shares that identity is shaped as "a person identifies with a set of characteristics and holds beliefs about his or her related performances" (Sauer, 2014). Scholar and feminist writer Sara Ahmed describes our identities as "the many factors that shape who we are" (Ahmed, 2018).

Our hearts call out a big YES to each definition. We view identities as the collection of characteristics, beliefs, circumstances, and personal truths that make up each one of us. Our identities are constructed from the ways others see us and the ways we see ourselves.

Some aspects of our identity are predetermined: the parts of ourselves we are born with—brown skin, green eyes, curly hair. Other layers of identity build up and change as we live our lives. They may be influenced by our families, friends, neighborhoods, and experiences. These layers of our identities can be made up of things such as interests, objects and places that bring us joy, family traditions, and spiritual beliefs and practices.

Why should we bring identity study into reading? When we don't think

Readers bring their own identities into their reading—their identities affect how they think about a story and what they learn from it.

about our own identities and study the identities of the characters, we lose the opportunity to create meaning and truly understand the characters in our books. This leads us back to Louise Rosenblatt's transactional reader-response theory, which teaches that there is never a singular meaning of a text. When the words on the page and our lives come together, we construct meaning. Simply said, who we are impacts how we see the characters in our books, what we think about them and their choices, and what lessons we pull from the pages. That meaning can even change over time because our identities are not static. This is often the reason why when we reread a book that has sat on a bookshelf for years, it touches us differently. We may connect with a different character or see motivation with new eyes—maybe because we now look through the eyes of a caregiver or of someone who has experienced deep and devastating loss.

Dana remembers experiencing this with Shel Silverstein's *The Giving Tree*. Her view of the character of the tree changed with life and her shifting identities. In her youth, Dana saw the tree as simple and weak. Then, through the eyes of a new mother, she understood the tree's desire to give the boy the world, even if it meant sacrificing everything. Now, as the mom of two middle schoolers, she has the urge to call out to the tree and will her the strength to say no. Nothing in this book has changed. But life has shifted Dana's view and, in turn, the meaning that she takes from its pages.

We also believe that centering our students' identities in our classrooms and our libraries will connect them to books and one another. During a visit with a fifth-grade class, Dana saw students "tasting" some picture books that they might read during their upcoming unit. When one little girl saw the beautiful book *The Proudest Blue* by Ibtihaj Muhammad and S. K. Ali, she yelled out, "I want this one. She looks just like me." Dana recalls the joy that radiated from this child's face as she saw someone on the book's cover who looked like her and her family. You may have a similar story of children who were drawn to books that offered them a mirror. Our book collections must capture the identities of our students and offer books with characters who have very different identities as well.

Throughout her childhood, Jigisha recalls scanning the library shelves in search of a story that would spark her interest and inspire a joy of reading. She saw other children open pages of a book and immediately immerse themselves in the story. Jigisha, however, never found stories that she could see herself in or feel a sense of belonging to, or books that had characters who even looked like her. Then, in Jigisha's fourth year of teaching, her school welcomed author Sarah Weeks, who had come to share her book *Save Me a Seat,* which she wrote with Gita Varadarajan. Weeks spoke about how her coauthor's own experiences inspired the experiences of the main character. People regularly mispronounced Varadarajan's name, and the author often felt pressure to fit into a culture and experience that was different from her own.

Jigisha realized that in her entire life she had never experienced a deep connection with a story, a character, and an author until then—when she was already in her 20s. She had finally found a book that not only reflected her own upbringing but also connected to her role as an educator. She had missed this type of immersive experience throughout her childhood. Moments such as these underscore the powerful impact such an experience can have for many children. A book brings shared experiences to life, and educators can spark that joy for many.

Reading through the lens of Identity will help readers see how their perspectives and selves impact the story they experience. And beyond that, as they consider the identities that the characters carry into their thinking, readers will push themselves to see the complexities of the people in their books. These complexities can help them make sense of someone's circumstance, desire, or decision.

Why Harm and Healing?

As we scan the books on our shelves, we'd be hard-pressed to find one that doesn't present a problem. Maybe it's because without challenge, there is no story. Maybe it's because our greatest successes often result from overcoming struggles. Maybe it's because harm and healing can set in motion the cycle of learning to be better.

The name of this section, specifically the word *harm*, may seem harsh. After all, the word itself means "physical or emotional injury." We spent quite a bit of time considering whether to revise the name of this lens. We revisited the language time and time again, asking ourselves if it was right for an elementary-focused book. We thought about other words, such as *hurt* or *problem*. Yet in the end, none of those words really captured the heart of this work. *Harm* is a harsh word, but it is also something that happens to all of us.

Being human means that we will experience harm. Sometimes a person may do us harm. At best, it is someone we don't know well. At worst, it is someone whom we love. There are even times when we harm ourselves. Other times, the norms and systems of our society or the realities of our circumstances cause us pain. In the end, we chose *harm* because there is a responsibility tied to that word that doesn't exist in words like *problem* or *hurt*. During our lives, we will all be harmed, and we will all carry the burden of being responsible for harming someone else. *Harm* is the right word, but in our title it doesn't stand alone. Right next to it is the word *healing*. This lens sets out to help children identify when harm happens and then study how people move forward to heal.

Raising a generation of people who will preserve our planet, respect one another, and create a better world requires that we teach our children to look for the causes of conflict, the repercussions of harmful choices, AND the ways we might heal the hurt we have caused. If we focus on the challenges characters experience and the ways they find a way forward to heal, we can help our readers deepen their understanding of the story and be moved to make different choices themselves.

Why Heartwork?

We exist in a world divided. Lines drawn come in many shapes and colors—based on politics, beliefs, and desires. It is easy to focus on our differences and to allow ourselves to "other" people around us. But we don't have to do that. In practicing perspective sharing and opening ourselves up to someone else's truth, we can begin to erase the lines that divide us and teach our children to do the same.

A NOTE ABOUT EMPATHY AND TEXT CHOICE

In her book *The Empathy Effect*, Dr. Helen Riess describes a phenomenon called *in-group bias*, or a preference toward those who share our physical characteristics. She explains that the roots of this bias stem from our ancestors living in tribes or small groups and depending on people within their group for survival. This in-group legacy becomes a problem when it limits our capacity to experience empathy for people who don't match up to any shared characteristics—the so-called "out-groups." "You may not even realize you have out-grouped whole segments of society, but all of us do" (Riess, 2018). While in-group bias is a truth we must deal with, it doesn't have to limit our students' ability to experience empathy. We can overcome these internal biases by bringing diverse groups of people into the lives of our students through the books we read and by teaching them strategies for practicing empathy. The need to overcome in-group bias is yet another reason why we must diversify our libraries.

Empathy is "when you feel someone's feelings in your own heart" (Mraz & Hertz, 2015). Taking it a step further, empathy is when we share someone's feelings and then react differently because we understand what they experience. The beauty of literacy is that we can marry literature with practicing empathy because reading mirrors and provides context for life and helps us understand the world and one another (Mar & Oatley, 2008). When we read, we share a heart with the characters. We feel the pain of having a best friend move away or being picked last for the kickball team. We experience the joy of baking bread with our grandmother or performing a solo in the recital. Reading and tuning in to the emotions of the characters and to our own reactions can provide emotional context and understanding.

Tucking in Universal Design for Learning (UDL)

The definitive objective for Universal Design for Learning (UDL) is for all children to transform into "expert learners" (CAST Learning Inc. 2018, cast.org). UDL provides educators with a lens of creating and implementing classroom structures in which all children have access and opportunities to the lessons and learning. This resource offers multiple entry points for both educators and learners through the power of stories and conversations. Through the lenses of Identity, Harm and Healing, and Heartwork, we offer children a chance to excel with lessons that offer engagement, representation, and expression. These lessons further align with UDL by leading children to engage in learning with purpose and motivation. When children hear stories about characters they can relate to and learn from, engage in conversations about understanding the characters' experiences and perspectives, and connect or extend their learning through circle conversations, we create moments that invite children to access and engage in learning. This further ensures that our lessons reduce barriers to learning and give students access to education.

All of us need strategies that we can use to support our learners. All of us need read-alouds and mentor texts. This book brings all those needs together, giving you everything you need to support the whole group as well as the personalized needs of your individual learners—plus serving as the perfect mentor text!

The Questions on People's Minds

Before we continue, let's take a few moments to address some people's concerns.

Aren't They Too Young?

For some educators, doing this work in K–2 classrooms is challenging because we, or others, question whether children in primary grades are too young for these conversations. Other educators wonder whether school is the place for these conversations to occur. However, researchers have proven that biases and prejudices begin early. We can see from children's behavior that they internalize societal messages about race (The Children's Community School, 2018; Tatum, 1997) and gender (Gender Justice in Early Childhood, 2017). These actions include friendship selection (e.g., choosing only friends who look like them, even in diverse classrooms and schools) and ascribing characteristics to specific identities (e.g., assuming people are more dangerous or less attractive based on skin color; assigning toys, roles, or clothing to a particular gender). Researchers have also found that even at an early age, children struggle with how the dominant culture ascribes goodness or beauty (Clark & Clark, 1947) or gender-appropriateness (Gender Justice in Early Childhood, 2017). These realities support the need to infuse early childhood education with antiracist and anti-bias instruction.

Since 1989, early childhood educator Louise Derman-Sparks has authored texts, individually and with others, that develop and help educators in teaching children to engage in anti-bias ways of being. In her most recent work, she and coauthors Julie Olsen Edwards and Catherine M. Goins state that their ultimate goal is "to support children's full development in our world of great human diversity and to give them the tools to stand up to prejudice, stereotyping, bias, and eventually to institutional isms" (Derman-Sparks, Edwards & Goins, 2020). The essence of Derman-Sparks's early childhood goals for anti-bias education—identity, diversity, justice, and activism—was used by the organization Learning for Justice to develop the social justice standards for Grades K–12.

What If They're (Almost) All White, or If They're (Almost) All BIPOC?

In the poster titled "If the World Was a Village of 100 People," researchers aligned visual images with 2020 statistics to show the diversity across humanity (DeBeaumont et al., 2021). A global economy, along with events such as natural disasters and wars, have increased the movement of populations over the last few decades. As a result, people today are likely to work—physically or virtually—with people who may not look like them. For this reason, cultural competence is a skill employers seek in both BIPOC and White job candidates. The growing diversity in public and suburban schools necessitates that White and BIPOC educators and students develop an appreciation for diversity as well as other SEL competencies and social justice skills needed to be empathetic, inclusive humans who are able to identify and push against oppressive forces. Indeed, the current social climate and state of democracy in the United States reflect a need for citizens who have experienced this type of education.

Don't These Conversations Make White Children Feel Shame and BIPOC Children Feel Inferior?

Feelings of inferiority and shame both center an individual's focus on self. When we center our focus on humanity, there is no reason for either. As creatures who evolved from prehistoric periods, during which our primitive brain needed to quickly read our environment to keep us safe from danger, we—BIPOC and White—are all prone to bias. We—White and BIPOC—are all socialized into ways of being that are affected by ideologies that predate our birth. We—BIPOC and White—are all born into a time period that came after centuries of humane and inhumane acts of commission and omission, which have empowered a few long-standing institutions to bestow rewards and punishment on the masses. These are ALL realities beyond our and our children's control. That means that neither they nor we—White or BIPOC—should feel shame or inferiority when we discover oppression in ourselves or learn truths about history that depict inhumane actions by people with whom we share class, ethnicity, language, nationality, race, or any other identity marker. Neither should we feel superior. We should not feel inferior nor superior—just human.

Shame is actually a barrier to the goals of this work as it can shut down the prefrontal cortex and force a person into fight or flight mode (Arnsten, 2015). Inferiority can have the same effect. This or any other response to stress can result in the opposite of a learning stance. Too frequently, this has been the reality for historically and culturally marginalized students who have suffered school-related trauma. Teachers who engage in culturally responsive and sustaining education, social justice, and anti-bias pedagogies—which all support social-emotional development— prevent and interrupt these types of Adverse Childhood Experiences (ACES) and set young learners of all identities on the path to stronger social-emotional competency. Curating a diverse collection of texts and intentionally drawing from it to design lessons about identity, diversity, justice, and action are effective tools that counter the narratives children learn about themselves and others in society. These tools also develop children's empathy, which is "the antidote to shame" (Brown, 2012) and is necessary to transform classrooms and schools into places of belonging, inclusion, and equity.

Now, let's take some time to think about how we approach this study and how our own identities play a role in our teaching.

LEARNING ABOUT OURSELVES

"It is critical to bear in mind that we cannot engage with our students around these issues when we have not engaged with our own selves. We have to know who we are and where we stand in order to have genuine and meaningful conversations with ourselves and others."
(Mentor & Sealey-Ruiz, 2021)

During the spring and summer preceding the 2020–21 school year, social-media platforms began to fill with educators' calls for "Maslow before Bloom." This was not just a mere suggestion to address students' basic human needs (Maslow) before expecting them to meet educational objectives. Aware of the stress and trauma resulting from the pandemic, educators demanded that we focus more on addressing children's social and emotional needs than on making up for their interrupted schooling.

Calls for SEL also resulted from the "racial reckoning" following the murders of Ahmaud Arbery, Breonna Taylor, and George Floyd. How do we do that? Given the lack of curricular connection to realities like this in most educational spaces, many acknowledged the need to implement SEL strategies with care, to avoid subjecting children to the "white supremacy with a hug" that Dena Simmons, educator and founder of LiberatED, has called out for several years (Madda, 2019; Simmons, 2019; Simmons, 2021).

Flash forward to 2023: After a year of book bans riding hand-in-hand with laws against critical race theory and/or historically and culturally marginalized authors or topics, especially those aligned to the LGBTQ+ community, Keisha expands Simmons's description of the concerns about SEL to include not just white supremacy but also "heterosexism with a hug." We should not implement a version of SEL that fails to acknowledge the many ways people identify and express their gender and sexual orientation. Although some people may think this addition unnecessary in primary and intermediate grades, we noted earlier that prejudices, biases, and stereotypes begin to form from an early age. Additionally, research cited by Gender Justice in Early Childhood (2017) suggests transgender and gender-expansive children self-identify as early as their toddler years. Based on this, we must do the self-work to make sure we and our learners develop the ability to be just to community members in and beyond our classrooms who represent the world's various identities.

As we attempt to provide children with support for SEL, we need to **avoid** practices that can inadvertently cause damage and **embrace** practices that celebrate the genius that is present in each child's identities. To do this, we educators must first tend to our own social-emotional learning. We all want to believe we are good people. However, social psychologist and author Dolly Chugh aptly argues that the frailty of humanity makes us, at best, "goodish" (2018), regardless of race, gender identity, or any other social identity marker.

To help us be better than "goodish," this section provides information to help strengthen adult skills, knowledge, and attitudes aligned with SEL and social justice. We recommend reading this section with a journal—physical or virtual—so you can record and review your thoughts, beliefs, and actions throughout and beyond this work. Educators with a growth mindset understand that the learning they do before, during, and after lessons is crucial, not only to their own sense of self-efficacy, but also to their students' learning and understanding. To fully develop the abilities needed to do this work, we need to understand an important aspect of our learning. That aspect is racial literacy.

Racial Literacy as a Mandatory Stance

In her book *The Dreamkeepers: Successful Teachers of African American Children,* Gloria Ladson-Billings expands the concept of pedagogy to include "noninstructional actions, such as smiling at a student or showing disapproval of a student" (2009). She then provides dimensions of culturally relevant teaching that paint a picture of a teacher who demonstrates this type of pedagogy. Such an educator:
   • sees herself as an artist and teaching as an art.
   • sees himself as part of the community and sees teaching as giving something back to the community; encourages children to do the same.
   • believes all students can succeed.
   • helps children make connections between their community, national, and global identities.
   • sees teaching as "pulling knowledge out"—like mining.

It is important to note that African American children are the focus of this seminal text, which unpacks culturally relevant teaching through research that involved actual teachers. But Black children are not the only beneficiaries of this pedagogy—it is relevant to all students, BIPOC and White as well. This is important to remember when considering the sociopolitical and cultural aspects of the tenets of culturally relevant teaching, as represented in the above characteristics. It also supports the earlier statements about the benefits of such teaching to all learners, whether they are historically and culturally marginalized or centered. This is because these tenets require even children who are traditionally centered to become dexterous in more than their own culture.

Culturally relevant teaching is foundational to both culturally responsive pedagogy (Gay, 2000) and culturally sustaining pedagogy (Paris & Alim, 2017). Both are strengths- or assets-based pedagogies that frame learners as sources of genius. Culturally sustaining pedagogy accentuates the facts that we live in a pluralistic society and that we should nurture and sustain—not extinguish—the rich cultures of BIPOC children through schooling. We can enact each of these pedagogies, and the others required to engage in the heartwork espoused in this book, only through ongoing and intentional development of racial literacy. Racial literacy encompasses several skills. It is "[t]he ability to read, recast, and resolve racially stressful encounters through the competent demonstration of intellectual, behavioral, and emotional skills of decoding and reducing racial stress during racial conflicts" (Stevenson, 2014).

Racial literacy, like all abilities, must be developed. Yolanda Sealey-Ruiz's theory of racial literacy development provides the theoretical framework for the heartwork put forth in this text. Educators must engage in the ongoing work of "excavating" themselves if they are to engage in antiracist and anti-bias teaching and learning with children. When it comes to the level of consciousness needed to do this work well, we cannot overstate the axiom "You cannot teach what you do not know." In areas related to and impacted by identities, we can teach destructive and affirming things intentionally and unintentionally. Therefore, to become racially literate, educators must engage in "a cyclical process of (re)examining perceptions, beliefs, and actions relating to race . . . [and] promote the idea of (de)constructing and (re)building a base for new perceptions founded on open-mindedness and understanding" (Price-Dennis & Sealey-Ruiz, 2021). The components of this process are critical love, critical humility, critical reflection, historical literacy, The Archaeology of Self™, and interruption. Table 2 (below) presents Sealey-Ruiz's definition for each term (Sealey-Ruiz, n.d.) along with some examples of how it relates to SEL and social justice.

Table 2: Racial Literacy Development

Component	Definition	Example (SEL and Social Justice Correlations)
Critical Love	A profound ethical commitment to caring for the communities we live in	Co-creating a community with learners that supports everyone in bringing their authentic selves to the classroom each day (Social awareness, relationship skills, and diversity, justice, and action)
Critical Humility	Remain open to understanding the limits of our own worldviews	Maintaining curiosity about and appreciation of differences (Social awareness, relationship skills, and responsible decision-making and diversity, justice, and action)
Critical Reflection	Think through the various layers of our identities and how our privileged and marginalized statuses affect the work	Seeking feedback from a fellow educator (e.g., coach, administrator, or grade-level colleague) or viewing a recording of a lesson to explore the ways you engage with historically and culturally marginalized students (Self-awareness, self-management, and responsible decision-making and diversity, justice, and action)

Historical Literacy	Develop a rich and contextual awareness of the historical forces that shape the communities in which we work, as well as the society in which we live	Taking the time to learn the systems and organizations in your school's community and how the supports they have or have not provided people have impacted the physical, social, emotional, and psychological safety of students and their families (Social awareness, relationship skills, and responsible decision-making and diversity, justice, and action)
The Archaeology of Self™	Deep excavation and exploration of beliefs, biases, and ideas that shape how we engage in the work	Analyzing the students recommended for intervention to determine if there are racialized patterns, and interrogating yourself to surface any beliefs or biases that might be directing you to implement pedagogies that do not support these learners (Self-awareness, social awareness, and responsible decision-making and identity, diversity, justice, and action)
Interruption	Interrupt racism and inequality at personal and systemic levels	Volunteering to be on data-focused school-level teams (e.g., Intervention and Referral Services Team and Positive Behavioral Interventions and Supports Committee) to support the collective identification of racialized patterns of underserving students through academic and disciplinary practices (Self-awareness, self-management, social awareness, and responsible decision-making and identity, diversity, justice, and action)

(Sealy-Ruiz, n.d.)

The Interconnectedness of SEL Competencies and Social Justice Standards

In December 2020, Karen Niemi, the president and CEO of the Collaborative for Academic, Social and Emotional Learning (CASEL), announced a revision of the "definition and framework to pay close attention to how SEL affirms the identities, strengths and experiences of all children, including those who have been marginalized in our education systems. CASEL has continued to highlight the importance of enhancing the social-emotional competence of all young people and adults, while putting additional emphasis on how we can all learn and work together to create caring and just schools and communities. . . . The updated language pays attention to personal and social identities, cultural competency, and collective action as part of SEL. It also emphasizes the skills, knowledge and mindsets needed to examine prejudices and biases, evaluate social norms and systemic inequities, and promote community well-being" (Niemi, 2020). Because of these changes, the five competencies of SEL and the Social Justice Standards now seamlessly fit together. Table 3 shows the broad connections between the two, and the following pages provide more details.

Table 3: Relationship Between SEL Competencies and Social Justice Standards (SJS)

CASEL		Learning for Justice
SEL Competency*	**Equity-Specific Competency**	**SJS Domain***
Self-Awareness	• Integrate personal and social identities • Identify personal, cultural, and linguistic assets • Examine prejudices and biases • Recognize beliefs**	**Identity**
Self-Management	• Set collective goals • Take initiative • Demonstrate collective agency	**Action**
Social Awareness	• Take others' perspectives • Recognize strengths in others • Show concern for the feelings of others • Identify diverse social norms, including unjust ones • Recognize situational demands and opportunities • Understand the influences of organizations/systems on behavior • Sense of belonging**	**Diversity** **Justice**
Relationship Skills	• Co-construction** • Demonstrate cultural competence • Practice teamwork and collaborative problem-solving • Stand up for the rights of others	**Diversity** **Justice** **Action**
Responsible Decision-Making	• Demonstrate curiosity and open-mindedness • Identify solutions for personal and social problems • Learn to make a reasoned judgment after analyzing information, data, facts • Reflect on one's role to promote personal, family, and community well-being • Evaluate personal, interpersonal, community, and institutional impacts • Distributive justice**	**Diversity** **Justice** **Action**

* CASEL's SEL Framework: What Are the Core Competence Areas and Where Are They Promoted?

** CASEL CARES Webinar Series: SEL as a Lever for Equity and Social Justice – Part II: Adult SEL to Support Antiracist Practices

*** Social Justice Standards: The Teaching Tolerance Anti-Bias Framework

The Relationship Between Self-Awareness and Identity

Self-awareness is all about identity. In an article psychologist and educator Beverly Daniel Tatum wrote more than two decades ago, she revealed what makes identity so intricate.

"The concept of identity is a complex one, shaped by individual characteristics, family dynamics, historical factors, and social and political contexts. Who am I? The answer depends in large part on who the world around me says I am. Who do my parents say I am? Who do my peers say I am? What message is reflected back to me in the faces and voices of my teachers, my neighbors, store clerks? What do I learn from the media about myself? How am I represented in the cultural images around me? Or am I missing from the picture altogether?" (Tatum, 2000)

Responding to these questions requires criticality, or the "ability to read texts (including print texts and social contexts) to understand power, authority and anti-oppression" (Muhammad, 2020). On its own, the question "Who am I?" takes a lifetime to figure out and often requires trustworthy and honest friends and therapists to facilitate the learning process. A huge part of the difficulty in answering this question lies in the fact that deep understanding of our self requires awareness of the situationally dependent ways in which the intersection of our social and personal identities may empower or disempower us. We will expand on this later, but it should be clear that surface-level thoughts about self-awareness are not sufficient. Taking the time to answer the questions Tatum presents in the previous paragraph will help us go deeply into the excavation process. Someone who is just beginning to focus on this type of adult learning might find it difficult to respond to all of Tatum's questions. Even a person who has engaged in deep excavation for years would have to take time to reflect on whether previous responses to each question may be different at this moment. But it is worth the time and effort to do this work.

 Take a moment to reflect on and respond to these questions.
- What thoughts do you have after reading Tatum's questions?
- How do these thoughts make you feel?
- Are there any questions you have answered before or could answer now without research (e.g., spending mindful and critical time noticing how media depicts people like you or conversing with a family member or friend)?
- If you don't feel ready to respond to all of Tatum's questions right now, to which questions do you feel you can respond? Underline or highlight those questions. What about the questions you are not prepared to answer at this time? You might write them in your journal along with a plan for how and when you might undertake the inquiry needed to begin answering those questions.

If you are comfortable answering any of the questions, take time now to do this in your journal. If, however, the questions seem too challenging at this stage of your journey, Table 4 presents a social-identity activity with prompts for reflection that may require less research.

In your journal, create a copy of Table 4 (below), leaving ample room in the last column to express your thoughts and feelings. Then follow these directions.

- Under "Your Social Identity," enter the identity you hold for the category in the first column.
- Under "Access/Barriers," note whether that identity provides access or barriers to opportunities and privileges.
- Under "Thoughts/Feelings," write your thinking about that aspect of your identity and your experiences with the accompanying access or barriers you have faced.

Table 4: Social-Identity Activity

Social Identity Category	Your Social Identity	Access/Barriers	Thoughts/Feelings
Ability (mental, physical, neurological)			
Age			
Biological Sex			
Class			
Education Level			
Ethnicity/Culture			
Gender Identity			
Gender Expression			
National Origin/Citizenship			
Race			
Relationship & Family Status			
Religion/Spirituality/Faith			
Sexual Orientation			
Size/Appearance			
Use of English/Other Languages			

Although the Social Identity Activity may be an easier starting point than the questions Tatum put forth, the last two columns may be time-consuming. The third column might even be a challenge that requires reading beyond this text. Reading an article like activist Peggy McIntosh's "White Privilege and Male Privilege: A Personal Account of Coming to See Correspondences Through Work in Women's Studies" (1988) might help inform your thinking.

Navigating Deeper Thoughts and Feelings

As shown in Table 2 (pages 17–18), self-awareness includes knowledge and understanding of prejudices and biases. Digging to this depth is challenging and necessitates a willingness to admit to and contend with self about the truths we uncover. We are more comfortable with admitting positive thoughts we think and positive things we do. We hold so tightly to these that we often struggle to admit, even to ourselves, that we have negative thoughts and feelings regarding some people, and even negative ways we treat some people. Because every person has learned certain ideologies, we all know negative stereotypes about people, including those like us. In addition to those thoughts that we can surface, there are thoughts that exist deep within our psyche—implicit or hidden—that contribute to our biases.

 Look back at Table 4 (page 21) and circle four categories. In your journal, create a copy of Table 5 (below), and then follow these directions.
- Under "Social Identity Category," list each of the four categories you circled.
- Under "Social Identities," list three identities that fall under the category for that row. For example, if you circled "National Origin/Citizenship," you might enter each of the following terms under this column: a. American citizen, b. immigrant, c. undocumented.
- In the next two columns, write three positive and three negative stereotypes for each of those identities. For example, you would write three positive stereotypes of American citizens next to "a" in the third column, and three negative stereotypes about American citizens next to "a" in the fourth column. You would then note stereotypes for immigrants after the letter "b," and so on.

Table 5: Stereotypes

Social Identity Category	Social Identities	Positive Stereotypes	Negative Stereotypes
1.	a. b. c.	a. b. c.	a. b. c.
2.	a. b. c.	a. b. c.	a. b. c.
3.	a. b. c.	a. b. c.	a. b. c.
4.	a. b. c.	a. b. c.	a. b. c.

After completing the table, think about how it felt to acknowledge the positive and negative stereotypes affiliated with different identities. Respond to the prompts below:

- Review each stereotype listed. Are you sure each is listed under the appropriate column— that it is indeed positive or negative? What evidence do you have that this labeling is true?
- Are you aware of the source or origin of any of these stereotypes?
- Which stereotypes represent beliefs you hold about people with the aligned identities? How do you feel about these beliefs?
- Do you think the stereotypes you believe affect your behavior, either positively or negatively, toward people with the aligned identities? What evidence do you have of this?

Keep in mind that it is highly probable that some of your responses to these questions may be incomplete or even untrue. As Chugh writes, "All of us have blind spots. In fact, if you find yourself thinking or saying, 'I don't think I have any blind spots,' then that is your blind spot" (2018). This means it is possible there are stereotypes we are unaware of knowing and believing, that we are possibly avoiding, hurting, favoring, or embracing some people because of unconscious beliefs. Remember that children's racialized and gendered socialization is observable at young ages. The ideologies of oppression, or *smog*, as Tatum calls it, exists, and we learn these ideologies with or without explicit instruction (Tatum, 1997; Husband, 2011; Harro, 2018). Therefore, we are affected by the smog whether or not we can identify it in and around us. Excavation specific to this area is vital as we need to surface how the oppressions in our world impact us to uncover the beliefs that guide our actions.

In her seminal text on the Historically Responsive Literacy Framework, Gholdy Muhammad writes, ". . . pedagogy must be viewed as both an art (imagination and creativity) and a science (theory, strategies, and methods of instruction). This approach calls for teachers to first unpack and make sense of their own histories and identities, which includes the ways they have used language and literacy practices in their own lives. In doing so, they must also unpack their own biases, assumptions, racisms, and other oppressive thoughts they have come to believe about people of color or other people whom others have marginalized" (Muhammad, 2020). It is important to note that the "imagination and creativity" Muhammad mentions are as affected by internal and external ideologies as the "theory, strategies, and methods of instruction" one selects. For these reasons, the *unpacking*, or self-excavation, is crucial. As put forth by Sealey-Ruiz in The Archaeology of Self™ (2021), we must maintain a stance of critical humility, believing there may always be more that we need to surface about ourselves. This will push us to continually interrogate our thinking and the beliefs that drive our actions. The Implicit Association Test (Project Implicit, n.d.) and the Implicit Bias Module Series (Kirwan Institute for the Study of Race and Ethnicity, 2018) provide opportunities to learn more about implicit bias and yourself.

The Relationship Between Self-Management and Action

In a 2017 TED Talk that expounds on his research into racial literacy, psychologist Howard C. Stevenson shares a recording of "the talk"—an actual conversation he had with his younger son, Julian. We recommend viewing "How to Resolve Racially Stressful Situations" (2017) to see a demonstration of Stevenson's racial literacy—the ways he assesses both his and his 8-year-old son's racial literacy and the ways he supports his son's racial-literacy development. He provides details that reveal his deep understanding of the ways stress affected his body during their conversation about the murder of Trayvon Martin and the acquittal of George Zimmerman. As Stevenson narrates his story, we can see how he works to not become dysregulated. To this talk, we can overlay Sealey-Ruiz's theory of racial literacy development (2021).

- **Critical love** – Stevenson made space for this important conversation with his son because he loves Julian and knows the emotional, mental, and physical safety of his son depends on his efforts to foster and nurture Julian's racial-literacy development. He makes sure to convey his love to his son verbally through remarks that provide a psychologically safe climate of belonging and culture of dignity. This encourages his son to share an incident of racial bias that he experienced at a pool and later challenge a perceived misunderstanding to ensure Stevenson understands that surviving a racialized act is most important.

- **Critical humility** – As a Black man, Stevenson is not only empathetic to his son's responses to this type of injustice but also has experienced the same types of reading of the world. Nevertheless, he refrains from inserting himself into his son's processing of the events. Instead, he speaks to validate and expand on his son's thoughts and feelings. Stevenson, a psychologist who has studied racial literacy for years, notes his own awkwardness at points in the conversation. This reflects his positioning of himself as a learner.

- **Critical reflection** – Stevenson's narration clearly shows that he is reflecting in the moment with his son and in the moment with his audience. Both demonstrate his ongoing practice.

- **Historical literacy** – In and beyond his conversation with his son, Stevenson grounds the talk in societal realities. He uses his son's processing of the 2013 report on the outcome of the trial against Trayvon Martin's murderer as a teachable moment.

- **The Archaeology of Self** – From the way Stevenson shares how he has unpacked his parents' different approaches to racism and acts of racialized prejudice to the way he reveals the visible and invisible processing he does during his conversation with his son, it is clear he continuously excavates himself. He mines the thoughts, feelings, and actions that overlay his experiences with himself, with others, and with the truths in the world. This excavating process helps Stevenson uncover the complexities within himself and improve his ways of being in the world.

- **Interruption** – The very act of developing racial literacy is an interruption. We posit that Stevenson's engagement in his own racial-literacy development was the catalyst to and is the sustenance for the research he executes in this area of his life, both personally and professionally.

Through the above analysis, we see the actions Stevenson took, consciously and unconsciously, to manage his emotions during the talk with his son. He used his skills in self-awareness to identify the emotions he felt. He then noted the places in his body that reacted to the rising stress. He supported this regulation of self by remaining mindful, which slowed and mitigated the evolutionary process of freeze-flight-fight. Stevenson's management of himself prevented his reptilian brain, or amygdala, from pushing his body into this freeze-flight-fight reaction. As a result, he could remain physically and mentally present to engage with his son in the difficult conversation. He maintained an active listening stance and a calm tone. He followed his son's lead and worked with him to rehearse their safest path if they were ever in a racialized and potentially violent situation.

 Think about how this connects to the heartwork we suggest in this book. Respond to the following questions in your journal. Be sure to include the emotions you feel as you reflect on each.

1. Have you ever heard a young child say any of the following?
   a. "Your skin looks like poop."
   b. "Why is that lady wearing that scarf over her face?"
   c. "You can't have two moms."
   d. "Girls can't play with trucks."

2. Have you ever said, or heard a colleague say, any of the following?
   a. "That name is too hard. Can I call you ___?"
   b. "Why do we have to find a place for them to pray?"
   c. "That's not a family."
   d. "Boys will be boys."

3. Do you have the courage to interrupt a child or an adult who makes any of these statements? If you are unsure or feel you do not, what would you need to find the courage to do so?

It is important to note the statements made by a young child are vocalizations of the child's attempts to understand the world. These are evidence of the smog (Tatum, 1997). We included these as well as adult statements to help you process them through the self-management skills needed to respond to such moments that may arise with children and/or adults. Taking the time to practice reading, recasting, and resolving each of these situations prepares you to respond in a mindful way when the actual moments arise. Reflecting on the moments after the fact, as Stevenson's example shows, helps you hone your skills so you are more equipped to respond to these situations on subsequent occasions.

The Relationship Between Social Awareness and Diversity and Justice

How do you perceive difference? In an essay written more than 20 years ago, Victoria Purcell-Gates stated:

". . . whether we interpret differences among children—or adults—as deficit or difference depends primarily on our preconceptions, attitudes toward, and stereotypes we hold toward the individual children's communities and cultures. If the child's family is poor, his parents undereducated, his dialect nonstandard, then we are much more likely to interpret experiential difference as a deficit in the child, in the parents, in the home, in the sociocultural community within which this child has grown up. And when we do this, we play God, conferring or denying educational opportunity to individual, socioculturally different, children. And we do not have the right to do this" (Purcell-Gates, 2002).

Too frequently, racial, class, and/or linguistic oppression result in patterns such as those described by Purcell-Gates. This is why we must continually engage in self-excavation and wrestle against those places within ourselves where oppressive beliefs dwell. Uncontested, internalized oppression seeps out through our practice in ways that "other" our learners and deny them the dignity they deserve. Our calls for "Maslow before Bloom" tend to focus more on the Maslowian levels of physiological and safety needs and not on love and belonging, esteem, and self-actualization. But social scientist Matthew Lieberman stated that mammals—which is what we are—enter this world dependent and need others to survive (Lieberman, 2014). He shared brain images that prove our brains register physical and social pain in the same way. Pain medication lessens the effects of both types of pain.

Based on this research, we know that our efforts to both interrogate and mitigate the negative impact of our biases and prejudices are crucial. If we do not take these actions, we might implement a pedagogy that "others" children who hold identities that have been historically and culturally marginalized. Following the logic in Bloom's hierarchy, these types of unintentional and intentional behaviors result in actions that do not raise these children's esteem and fulfill their cognitive needs. If they are to thrive, every one of our students needs to feel they belong and have worth in the fullness of any identities they hold. Feeling a sense of belonging means each child, regardless of identities, feels "appreciated, validated, accepted, and treated fairly within an environment (e.g., school, classroom, or work)" (Cobb & Krownapple, 2019). The creators of this definition of belonging go on to define *dignity* as "the innate, equal worth of each human being simply because that person is human . . . our common heritage and birthright as human beings."

Following the maxim that "you can't pour from an empty cup," we cannot teach social awareness if we are not aware of society's impact on ourselves. The critical love and critical humility needed to empathize with learners who may be different from our own self require thinking about other aspects of ourselves that affect how we show up for ourselves and others.

Consider and journal responses to the following questions as well as any emotions that arise.

- How validated do you feel at work? at home?
- How appreciated do you feel at work? at home?
- How accepted do you feel at work? at home?
- How fairly are you treated at work? at home?

These four questions, loosely aligned to the Indicators of Belonging put forth by Cobb and Krownapple (2019), indicate both the extent to which one's dignity is being honored and the extent to which one feels like they belong in each of their environments. Based on your responses, do you feel your dignity is honored at work and in your home? Similarly, do you feel like you belong at work and in your home? If you answered "no" to either of these questions, how does that make you feel? How might you manage those feelings in ways that impact how you show up in the classroom?

Now, change the questions to consider the experiences of belonging and dignity from the perspective of each child in your classroom whom you consider to be like you. Next, using those same four questions, shift to focus on the perspective of each child whom you think holds any identity that is different from your identities.

 Here are examples of reframed questions:

- How validated does Julissa feel in our classroom? in the cafeteria? on the playground? at home?
- How appreciated does Kareem feel in our classroom? in the cafeteria? on the playground? at home?
- How accepted does Tai feel in our classroom? in the cafeteria? on the playground? at home?
- How fairly is Miguel treated in our classroom? in the cafeteria? on the playground? at home?

Further questions you may ponder include:
- Is Hana worthy of your love, dignity, and affection simply because she exists? Or does Hana have to earn your love, dignity, and affection? Why?
- How does Zev experience your pedagogy?
- Do you welcome or avoid Alejandro's parents/caregivers? Why?

As you attempt to do this journaling, consider the evidence that exists to support your perspective for each of the responses for each child. Are the supports for your thoughts based on your beliefs, or do you have objective evidence? Applying the skills you have been honing through journaling, are there any truths you may not be able to see yet because you are still learning to excavate and mitigate your prejudices, biases, and beliefs? Consider the systems that operate in your classroom/school and how they may affect historically and culturally marginalized children. Are there any gaps between what you think you understand about these systems and how these systems affect the ways in which marginalized children are taught? What could be the unintended effects of those gaps? Your responses to these questions reveal the extent to which the classroom and school in which your students are learning are just. While the diversity of our classrooms and schools is often, though not always, beyond our control, identifying unjust practices and taking on the responsibilities to interrupt them is within our power.

To best teach lessons like those aligned to the lenses we put forth in this book, educators should learn more about the community in which they teach as well as the national and global society. One way to do this is to expand our historical literacy by reading texts about histories too often excluded from our educational experiences. Additional activities that can support this learning include conducting home visits at least once each year (these can be virtual family visits, pending social-distancing restrictions) and participating in community activities your students and their families enjoy. Maintaining a learning stance by engaging with curiosity interrupts the evolutionary tendency to become fearful of the unknowns that could trigger a freeze-flight-fight response. Maintaining a learning stance increases racial literacy and strengthens our capacity to execute the pedagogies needed for heartwork.

The Link Between Relationship Skills and Diversity, Justice, and Action

"Relationships are the heart of equity; belonging is the beat and rhythm that shows its vitality; and dignity is the blood that enlivens it." (Cobb & Krownapple, 2019).

Relationship skills best demonstrate that the competencies of SEL are interconnected and interdependent. Human connection requires each person to be self-aware, to manage their "self," to be socially aware, and to make decisions responsibly. To best connect with a student, an educator needs to know their self and ascribe worth to the child. This means we cannot be ability-evasive, color-evasive, culture-evasive, or gender-evasive. As described earlier, we have to acknowledge each and every aspect of the child's identities and view each as an asset that contributes to the genius the child holds. Diversity exists in most of our classrooms. In all our classrooms, relationships require children to feel included. According to Cobb and Krownapple, "[i]nclusion is engagement within a community where the equal worth and inherent dignity of each person is honored. An inclusive community promotes and sustains a sense of belonging; it affirms the talents, beliefs, backgrounds, and ways of living of its members" (2019).

To be an engaged learner, a child must be able to safely show up as their full, authentic self and take risks. Children do not leave their culture outside the classroom. Author and educator Sonia Nieto characterizes culture as "dynamic; multifaceted; embedded in context; influenced by social, economic, and political factors; created and socially constructed; learned; and dialectical" (1999). Therefore, a classroom's culture cannot be one of dignity unless we ascribe worth to all of the cultures that enter the room with our students. A classroom environment that supports this must be psychologically safe to reward vulnerability. Vulnerability is "the birthplace of love, belonging, joy, courage, empathy, and creativity. It is the source of hope, empathy, accountability, and authenticity" (Brown, 2015). Vulnerability allows learners to attain the higher levels of Bloom's taxonomy—analyzing, evaluating, and creating. Table 6, which is adapted from a list of vulnerable behaviors generated by Leader Factor (n.d.), lists many of the learning behaviors that are enabled by a psychologically safe environment. As stated above, an environment that does not provide a child with belonging does not provide that child with the climate and culture needed to reach the evaluating and creating levels of cognition.

Table 6: Acts of Vulnerability

Admitting a mistake	Saying "I don't know"
Asking a question	Saying "no"
Asking for help	Sharing an alternate point of view
Challenging the status quo	Sharing an idea
Disagreeing	Sharing something personal
Doing something you're not good at . . . yet	Sharing your emotions
Giving feedback	Trying something new

(Adapted from Leader Factor, n.d.)

Cobb and Krownapple define *climate* as "the feel of an environment" and go on to add, "Do people feel like they belong? Can they call their environment their own? Or do they feel alienated?" (2019). They define *access* as "the ability to have opportunities equal to those of other people." Keisha recalls visiting a carceral, or prison-like, kindergarten classroom in which all the Black and Brown boys were not seated at the tables with the other learners but were at desks on the periphery of the room. These boys of color had to earn their way back to the community of learners. How much do you think these boys of color, relegated to the periphery of the classroom, felt like they belonged? How much dignity could these boys feel? How much could these boys trust the teacher and instructional aide in the class? How much psychological safety could these boys experience? How just was this class?

Consider whether these boys of color felt as though they could safely take the risks learning requires. Full engagement in the classroom demands that children not simply be in the room but be considered an integral part of the learning community. Children should not have to earn this position; it should be their right as members of the classroom. For this to become the boys' reality, their teacher would not only have to unpack the biases she holds regarding boys of color but also acknowledge all the identities each boy holds to highlight the strengths each brings into the classroom. As a goal of this self-work, the teacher would need to surface and confront her beliefs that led to each boy's banishment and take steps to become a teacher who deserves the trust of each student. Doing so would mean holding herself accountable—and possibly enlisting the help of the instructional aide or a coach as an accountability partner—for the work needed to develop and maintain a classroom environment in which each learner experiences psychological safety.

As we've mentioned earlier, the characteristics of social-emotional learning are interdependent. To successfully demonstrate relationship skills, one needs to also be self- and socially aware, manage their self, and make responsible decisions. At its simplest, this requires:

- knowing, examining, and mitigating one's triggers (which are impacted by prejudices and biases);
- "demonstrating empathy and compassion" (CASEL, 2020) to another regardless of differences; and
- realizing one's own influence on another in a relationship.

These capacities are required to be culturally competent—an ability needed to be in a relationship with another. Due to the interconnectedness across characteristics, teachers should view challenges in developing healthy relationships with children as evidence of learning they have yet to master. They should work to determine the relationship skills they need to develop, along with other SEL characteristics they might need to strengthen first. Relationship skills are also strengthened by developing the components in Sealey-Ruiz's Racial Literacy Development theory: critical love, critical humility, critical reflection, historical literacy, the Archaeology of Self, and interruption (see page 17).

The Relationship Between Responsible Decision-Making and Diversity, Justice, and Action
"We do not really see through our eyes or hear through our ears, but through our beliefs. To put our beliefs on hold is to cease to exist as ourselves for a moment—and that is not easy. It is painful as well, because it means turning yourself inside out, giving up your own sense of who you are, and being willing to see yourself in the unflattering light of another's angry gaze. It is not easy, but it is the only way to learn what it might feel like to be someone else and the only way to start the dialogue" (Delpit, 2006).

Similar to relationship skills, responsible decision-making draws on other SEL competencies and is strengthened by racial literacy development. A person who is able "to make caring and constructive choices about personal behavior and social interactions across diverse situations" (CASEL, 2020) has to understand their positionality, or the ways their historically and/or culturally marginalized identities intersect and affect their decision-making and those impacted by their decisions. This necessitates a complicated and challenging excavation of self- and social awareness that Lisa Delpit's words help explain. This Archaeology of Self forces each person to unearth the ways they show up and the why behind those ways by making the self an object of deep, ongoing study.

Our natural inclination is to interpret every situation through our own lens. We hold academic, behavioral, cultural, gendered, linguistic, and physical expectations for others based on our ways of being. We read others' academic, behavioral, cultural, gendered, linguistic, and physical performances through our ways of being. If we have not interrogated these truths, we can either miss or inflate the data we glean from others' ways of being. Whether under- or overvalued, the error negatively impacts the decisions we make and our enactment of educational justice. In the classroom, this can lead to prison-like discipline practices, like those Keisha observed in the kindergarten classroom described earlier. Biased or prejudiced readings of others can also result in pedagogical practices and curricular choices that are ableist, heteronormative, racially intolerant, religion intolerant, and/or xenophobic.

For example, Keisha identifies as a Black, fat, English-speaking, cisgender, heterosexual, multiple-degreed, female American citizen. As such, she has to remain curious about the stories of others (e.g., students, family and community members, and colleagues) whose ways of being may not be like hers. She also must consider how differences between her and others affect her decisions as well as how those decisions affect others. Below are examples of culturally responsive decisions Keisha made as a classroom teacher.

- Integrated children's and families' funds of knowledge and ways of being into the taught curriculum whenever possible.
- Took the time to know parents and welcomed them into the classroom to share aspects of their culture.
- Sought out texts, realia, and other ways to represent children and their homes in the classroom.
- Interrupted gendered expectations and teasing in children's play.
- Co-created classroom expectations with children.
- Used her limited, conversational Spanish as much as possible with parents who depended on their children to interpret, and sought interpreters for oral and written communication as often as possible.
- Acknowledged the unease she felt with a child who did not make eye contact, accepted that she would need to unlearn eye contact as the expected behavior when talking with someone, and relearned averted eyes as a behavior to expect from some children (and adults) based on their cultural ways of being.

 There are many culturally responsive decisions a classroom teacher can make. Think of decisions you have made as a teacher. Then, respond to the questions below and reflect on the reason for each decision you have made.

- What were your teachers' expectations of how children should perform in each of the following categories: academic, behavioral, cultural, gendered, linguistic, and physical?
- Which of these aligned with the expectations of the adults at your home? Which did not align? How did you feel about expectations that did not align? How were you treated by the teacher? Other adults? Your classmates?
- Were there any students for whom there appeared to be a mismatch between an expectation and how the child performed? If so, what do you recall about the way the student(s) were treated by the teacher? Other adults? Your classmates? You?

- How have expectations that aligned with your home informed your own classroom rules? How have expectations that did not align informed your classroom rules?
- What are your expectations of the ways children should perform in each of the following categories: academic, behavioral, cultural, gendered, linguistic, and physical?
- Are there any students for whom there appears to be a mismatch between an expectation and how the child performs? If so, what do you notice about the way the student(s) are treated by you? Other adults? Their classmates?
- For each child whose performance suggests there is alignment between your expectations and those of their adults at home, what messages have you "read" about their family? For each child whose performance suggests there is no alignment between your expectations and those of their adults at home, what messages have you "read" about their family?
- How have you unearthed each of your students' ways of being? How are the cultures of each of your students reflected in the texts, realia, and other resources and materials you use for instruction? How are they reflected in the materials that are in your room but not used for instruction?
- Have you conducted a home visit, home survey, and/or interview with each family? If so, how frequently?
- Have you administered a student survey and/or interview? If so, how frequently?

These questions are by no means exhaustive. Additionally, your answers to these may not be the same from year to year, even if you remain in the same school and the same classroom. In any given year, however, your answers to these and other questions are reflected in the ways you manage your classroom, design your lessons, engage parents, and distribute resources (including 1:1 time with you). Each action involves multiple decisions. As you engage in the self-work to increase just practices in your classroom, the work you do will have a ripple effect: Critical love will compel you to advocate for just practices to increase for the children beyond your room.

Continuing "The Work"

As this section concludes, we hope it is clear that self-work doesn't end here. It should also be evident that SEL and social justice are interdependent and reciprocal. Skills in one often build from skills in the other, and developing skills in one often strengthens skills in the other. This is especially true when we intentionally connect self-development to racial-literacy development because of the multiple ways we are knowingly or unknowingly impacted by race through racialized systems, such as justice. Understanding this along with how other social constructs—such as class, gender, ethnicity, language, nationality, race, and religion—affect us is lifetime work. We are all products of histories most of us have never been taught. This is why we must do the excavating of ourselves even while we learn the social, including familial, ways we have come to be as we are. As we bring the outcomes of the excavations into our practice, we uncover ways we have grown and ways we still need to grow to impact our students, schools, and communities in a positive way.

LEARNING ABOUT OUR PRACTICES

In this section, you will find a guide to implementing the teaching work within each lesson—from using strategies in whole-class mini-lessons and comprehension conversations to meeting the needs of each child in one-on-one conferences. The lessons are not meant to be followed as scripts, nor do we expect you to do the mini-lesson, conduct the circle, or follow up with conferring conversations with these strategies in mind. Think of the book's lessons as a choose-your-own-adventure exercise. If your intention is to provide children with another strategy in their pocket, you might decide to bring the strategy into a mini-lesson or small group. If your intention is to explore an idea more deeply as a classroom community, you might choose to use the circle portion. To reiterate, this is not a script. It is a toolbox of possibilities with examples and suggestions. Make the teaching and language your own!

Strategies, Steps, and Storytelling

You might equate strategies to the little recipe cards you get in those ready-to-go meals by mail. As you lift the lid, you find all the ingredients and a set of sequenced directions that enable even a novice chef to create a gourmet meal in 20 minutes or less. For readers, strategies act as the recipe for what to notice or ask themselves. Each mini-lesson provides a strategy that teaches readers one way they can expand how they think about books, easy-to-follow steps to make the strategy tangible and clear, and places to pause in the book where teachers can model their thinking process and how it helps them as a reader.

The Places to Pause sections in our mini-lessons are the "I do" teacher think-aloud work of gradual-release teaching. These sections offer examples of possible think-alouds that will bring the strategy to life. Of course, these are just examples of how thinking across the steps of a strategy might go. Feel free to change up the suggestions to match them to your own ideas and observations. That said, don't skip the model! Steps are great; but showing children strategies in action is necessary before we can ask them to try out the work.

While we model strategies in front of our students, it is easy to fall into the trap of asking children for their "help" through the process. Questioning as we model the strategies may seem like a good way to keep our young readers engaged. What often happens, however, is that the back-and-forth questioning makes it hard for children to follow the process, and so they don't see a smooth and clear example of a strategy in action.

Tips on Effective Strategy Instruction

Strategy instruction and modeling work can be used inside many different literacy components. We might tuck strategies into our interactive read-alouds, make them the star of the show in whole-group mini-lessons, or bring them into targeted small-group reading instruction or individual conferences. No matter where they turn up in your teaching, our Top 10 Tips for Strategy Instruction can help lift the level of your strategy work.

TOP 10 TIPS FOR STRATEGY INSTRUCTION

1. Name the strategy and its purpose before you begin modeling.

2. Break down what you're doing into a how-to process with steps.

3. Begin each step with a verb to make sure it is actionable.

4. Intentionally add pauses within your think-alouds to demonstrate that all readers need thinking time.

5. Refer to parts of the book throughout your modeling to show how your thinking grows from the strategy and the book.

6. During modeling, help children focus on YOUR process by avoiding questions and doing all of the talking.

7. Be clear with the steps by using phrases such as "First, I . . . ," "Next, I . . . ," and "Last, I . . ." or lifting your fingers as you teach each step.

8. When thinking aloud, use language such as "Maybe" or "One possibility" to model that there are many ways to answer.

9. Write the strategies on charts so children can refer to them as needed during their independent reading.

10. Be flexible by allowing children to change up the strategy. The goal is thinking, rather than a perfect match to your step.

Balancing Steps and Story

Clear and explicit strategy instruction can provide children with a pathway to success (Serravallo, 2010, 2015; Goldberg, 2016; Hattie, 2018). However, finding the right balance between clarity and a human touch can be challenging. Reading is a personal experience, so we must be careful not to turn our thinking into a set of robotic steps that feels too much like reciting that recipe card rather than teaching. You can avoid the robot-teacher act by genuinely pausing to consider the thoughts that go through your mind and referring to those little bits of the page and picture that brought you to a realization. The best modeling sounds like storytelling our process with a smile.

Another goal for our strategy work is to ensure that our process is transferable and replicable. That leaves us to plan our instruction with an intentional mix of a clearly named strategy in transferable language, its purpose, steps that offer a process for how children might put that strategy into practice, and a bit of modeling that helps them see our steps in action through storytelling our internal thinking.

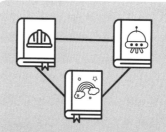

STRATEGIES THAT WORK IN ANY BOOK

To help children understand that strategies can be transferred from book to book, take book-specific language out of the steps and replace that language with general literacy terms. For example:

Instead of: *Think about how the puppy is feeling right now after the little boy yelled at him.*

Try this: *Think about what just happened to the character. Look at his face. Ask yourself, "How might he feel right now?"*

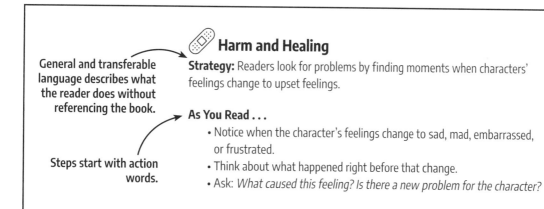

General and transferable language describes what the reader does without referencing the book.

Steps start with action words.

Harm and Healing

Strategy: Readers look for problems by finding moments when characters' feelings change to upset feelings.

As You Read . . .
- Notice when the character's feelings change to sad, mad, embarrassed, or frustrated.
- Think about what happened right before that change.
- Ask: *What caused this feeling? Is there a new problem for the character?*

Classroom Close-Up: Mini-Lesson

This Classroom Close-Up provides an example of strategy work in action during a whole-class mini-lesson. Note: We do not save strategies for mini-lessons alone. We offer strategies as entry points to trying skills during mini-lessons, small-group instruction, conferences, and countless other classroom experiences. Strategies are simply pathways to try out a chosen skill or goal. In this lesson, you'll notice Dana does most of the talking. That is because in a mini-lesson the intention is to clearly model a strategy without any back-and-forth questioning that can distract children from smoothly seeing the steps in action. After modeling, we offer children an opportunity to try out that strategy with a quick turn-and-talk. The lesson takes no more than 10 minutes—a quick in and out to highlight one way of thinking about books.

This lesson features a group of first graders exploring Harm and Healing work through the book *Zonia's Rain Forest,* by Juana Martinez-Neal (see page 126). Six and 7-year-olds scramble to their carpet spots as Dana settles into a rocking chair next to the classroom easel.

Dana: Hello, Readers! I know you saw Zonia back up here on the easel and are excited to visit her story again! Today, as we revisit Zonia, let's go back to some of our Harm and Healing thoughts. We know that sometimes we can learn messages from the stories we read. One great way to find those messages is by focusing on a part that shows a problem and then asking questions that begin with *who, how,* and *why.* Let's try it out. I'm going to name a problem I see the characters are dealing with and ask questions like: *Who is affected by this? How does it affect them? What do they do?* And then I am going to think about a message that comes from answering those questions.

Dana opens the book to the page that shows Zonia telling her mom about finding the destroyed section of forest.

Dana: We all remember this part, right? It's right after Zonia sees the burned-down trees. Thumbs up if you remember.

Children hold up their thumbs high in the air and nod their heads furiously.

Dana: This was sad. Okay. Let's try out some thinking. I want to think about a message. Let me first think about the problem. Well . . . The problem here is that the trees were gone and the forest was destroyed. Now, I'm going to ask myself some questions: Who is affected by this? *(Dana pauses to think.)* Well, let's see. It definitely affects Zonia. She's upset about the trees being destroyed. *(Dana pauses again.)* It also affects the animals in the forest. Now, let me try another question: How does this hurt them? *(Another pause. Dana rubs her chin to show that she wants to consider this for a moment.)* It seems like the forest being destroyed hurts them because they're all losing part of their home. What do they do? Well, Zonia says she's going to help. So let me think about a message. *(Dana pauses one last time to show some thinking time.)*

Maybe a message from this book is that we all need to help care for the Earth and that we are responsible for fighting against the things that hurt it. Did you see how I used the questions to help me find a message?

Dana transitions from modeling and invites children to engage with a different book they've previously read. She picks up the book *A Sled for Gabo,* by Emma Otheguy, from the basket next to her chair.

Dana: Now, it's your turn to try this out. I know you all remember this book. This is another favorite! Right now, think about the big problem in the story. When you have it, put your thumb up in the air. *(Dana pauses to wait for thumbs to go up.)* Now, try out some questions. Ask: *Who is affected by this problem? How? Who is around to help? What do they do?* You can make up your own questions, too. Put up your other thumb when you've got a question or two. *(Dana pauses again.)* Okay, now ask yourself those questions and squeeze your brain to think about how the answers can lead you to a message from the book. Wiggle your fingers in the air when you have answered your question and you have a message.

When the carpeted area looks like a sea of raised hands and wiggling fingers, Dana prompts children to turn and talk. Chatter fills the room. As children share their ideas, Dana circulates, listening and coaching for a couple of minutes. Some children talk about the boy being shy. They ask questions, such as: *How did this hurt him? What did he do to make a friend?* They came to messages, such as: "Sometimes you need a little push to make a friend." Other children talk about Gabo not having a sled to play with. They ask questions, such as: *What did that stop him from doing? Who helped him?* They came up with messages, such as: "You can always find a way to play and have fun."

After a couple of minutes, Dana calls the children's attention and shares that she'd heard wonderful questions that led children to find all kinds of great messages from the book. She shares a couple of examples that she'd heard while coaching them. To finish up the lesson, Dana reminds children that they could use this strategy in lots of other books.

Dana: Let's remember that our books do more than tell stories about characters; they can also send us messages. If you are trying to find a message from one of your books, you can always try to find the problem, ask some *who, how, what,* and *why* questions, and then see if your answers lead you to a message!

Using Circle Questions and Prompts

After reading a book, we want children to dive into productive, deep conversations about its ideas. Because such dialogue doesn't always happen, we need tools to lean on. One of the best tools we know of to get children to think, contribute, and listen is using "circles."

Circles: What and Why

Circles are a structure people use to come together as a community. We gather children in the form of a circle, pose a question or prompt, and then invite them to contribute their ideas and perspectives to the whole community.

Circles and classroom conversation certainly have overlapping goals; however, the format and the benefits of each remain different. In general, circles are not intended as a back-and-forth exchange. Instead, they provide a space where everyone has an opportunity to voice their idea while others listen. See the similarities and differences between circles and conversations below.

Conversations
- Talk moves back and forth between children as they think of responses
- Children agree or disagree
- Children may try to prove their points are correct or find a better stance

- Children listen to hear other perspectives
- Raising hands isn't necessary

Circles
- Every person is intentionally invited to contribute
- Circle protocol sets clear guidelines and norms
- Children reflect on the different perspectives and ideas shared by the whole group

Using circles for communication and connection is not a new idea. Circles have ancient roots in many indigenous cultures. The circular gathering of people in ceremony, dance, mourning, and celebrations allows us to truly be with one another. To share a heartbeat. When we gather as a circle, we become one unit. Circles do more than provide a space for us to sit. They are a living symbol that provides a message of equality, safety, responsibility to one another, and connectedness (Costello, Wachtel & Wachtel, 2019). There is no leader or follower, and all social hierarchy is left behind as we face one another. The unity created in this configuration is the reason circles are broadly used today in recovery, therapies, prayer groups, and, now, in schools.

As literacy teachers, we have been thinking about how we can use circle practices to enhance our reading and conversational work. We have spent decades dreaming about rich whole-class discussions. We have been striving for such rich whole-class discussions, and yet they often have fallen short of fabulous. The reality in our classrooms—and in the classrooms of many other teachers we've worked with—is that when we are in a whole-group situation, a few children carry the entire conversation. The quieter voices never reach the surface, and the gift of their would-be contributions is lost.

For years, our solution was to utilize turn-and-talk or think-pair-share practices, in which everyone had a partner or two and could share their ideas huddled up in their little groups. This allowed for children to feel more comfortable while also inviting the whole group to try, think, and engage. But it did not allow contributions to reach the whole class community. Many voices never made it beyond their little groups and, as a result, their perspectives did not fully move, inspire, or challenge the community. Don't get us wrong. Turn-and-talk is still and forever will be a favorite technique for engaging children in trying out a strategy or exploring some thinking. But when our goal is to benefit from the collective knowledge present in the room, circles are a better choice to embody that practice.

Building Relationships Before Book Talks

Whether handing over a piece of our writing to peers or simply sharing our thoughts with a group, truly showing up is, in many ways, reminiscent of that horrible nightmare in which we end up at school in our underwear. We can't move too quickly into a space of vulnerability. If we do, children will meet us with resistance that shows up as avoidance, silence, or distraction (Nathanson, 1994).

Expecting someone to open up and share their fears, thoughts, and deepest desires can't happen in the first go-round. As a matter of fact, if that kind of sharing does happen too early, it will surely result in what author and educator Brené Brown calls a *vulnerability hangover* (2012). We've all been there. It feels like the morning-after effect—that stomach-plunging moment when you wake up and remember the conversation with an acquaintance that somehow led you to open up and reveal a deep, dark secret you thought was buried so deep it could never surface, especially not with someone you barely know. Whether due to moments of lowered inhibitions or simply because you felt overly comfortable in the moment, opening up too quickly makes us want to burrow back under the covers and hide forever.

> **GETTING-TO-KNOW-YOU PROMPTS AND QUESTIONS**
> - Do you prefer ___ (e.g., cookies or chips, crayons or markers, sunshine or puddles)?
> - Where would you like to go for a vacation?
> - What do you think of when I say ___ (e.g., green, heart, thunderstorm)?
> - What is your favorite thing to play?
> - What makes you smile?
> - What makes you frown?
> - What scares you?
> - Who or what are you grateful for?

One way to avoid the vulnerability hangover is simply to go slow and start the school year by building trust. In your first circle series, stay safe in the shallow water. Begin building this work through the practices of community building in morning meetings. Focus early circles on simple getting-to-know-you type of questions that feel playful and don't reach too far into deeply emotional topics.

Once we've built a strong classroom community, the reasons for circling may shift. In our mini-lessons, we offer circle questions and prompts that support reading and social comprehension. How you conduct the circles, however, is up to you.

There are a few different ways you can implement circles. In the pages that follow, we'll explore the types of circle and conversational structures we use in our practices and the benefits they offer to literacy learners.

Sequential and Nonsequential Circles

During **sequential circles**, we provide children with a question or prompt to consider. Then, going around the circle, either clockwise or counterclockwise, each child adds his or her contribution to the community. (When we engaged in remote-learning experiences, we conducted these same circles by creating a class list that was visible to all the children and moved up or down the list.) Of course, if children are not ready to contribute, they have the option to pass. But our hope is that we have created such a deep sense of comfort in our circles that children will be willing to take a risk and offer up their ideas. Sometimes a child may pass because he or she needs additional thinking time, so we revisit all the children who have passed at the end of the first go-around. This offers them a second chance to bring their thoughts forward. The benefit of a sequential circle is the comfort that comes with knowing when you're going to be invited to contribute.

Nonsequential circles also invite every child to add their contribution; however, these circles do not suggest any particular order. Children who engage in these experiences might simply listen to one another and step forward to contribute when they are ready and there is a quiet space. When they finish sharing, they step back and leave an opening for another child to join in. The benefit of using a nonsequential circle is that children have the freedom to choose when they add their ideas to the community. Those who may need more time to think can give themselves the space to become inspired in a less conspicuous manner.

An alternate form of nonsequential circles that many children enjoy uses a framework in which the last contributor invites another child to step forward. The contributor may hand a "talking piece" to someone else in the group or invite a new person by name. There is something beautiful about having someone say our name and invite us to bring our thoughts

ESTABLISHING NORMS FOR CIRCLES

While we play together and slowly open up, we also need to begin establishing clear norms for our community. Coauthoring norms for circles allows children to feel safe sharing their thinking and is much more powerful than having the teacher name the rules of the circle. We might start by explaining to children why circles will be a part of our class community and introduce some general truths about the need for making circles a safe space. We acknowledge that, at times, teachers may decide to begin by offering examples that can be revised with children. If so, here are some common guidelines that can get you started:

• Speak from the heart.

• Listen with respect.

• Speak with respect.

• Share just enough.

• Stay in the circle.

While starters can be helpful for some as we begin the journey, remember that as community norms, children should have some authorship and ownership, even if only through revision. Whether starting from scratch or revising together, here are some questions to support coauthoring circle norms:

• What would a successful circle look like? Sound like?

• What do I need from myself in the circle?

• What do I need from my circle mates?

to the surface. This invitation lets us know that our thoughts are valued and that they have a place here in the community.

As you can imagine, although they are in different forms, all these structures feel more like a sharing session than a conversation. Our goal in these experiences is to allow every voice to be heard and to collect the thoughts and perspectives of the entire group.

Children reflect on what a classmate shared during a circle.

Before conducting sequential or nonsequential circles, be sure to set expectations for children that would allow for a successful experience. We want them to feel ready and have a clear understanding of the length of responses. Finding the right balance in timing can be tricky because while we want every voice heard, we also must be mindful of time and children's ability to stay focused. These sharing circles may call for just a few words or sentences per person. In our experience, younger children do well with shorter responses or sentence stems.

When gathering into the circle, spend the first few moments restating the established norms, that day's timing or response length goals, and then offer the question followed by a moment of silent thinking time. If you have a particularly deep prompt, you may even allow children to think and jot ideas about the prompt before coming to the circle. Having time to dig deep into their hearts and minds can help children feel confident about their contributions.

Fishbowls

Another type of circle configuration is the **fishbowl**. Imagine a fishbowl. Its walls make it a sturdy container, while the fish inside flit about their domain, full of energy and life. In our classroom version, the children in the inner circle are the focus, much like the fish. This is where the action is—where children share, explore, or look for support. The children in the outer circle, like the wall of the bowl, remain still. They are listeners and learners. Fishbowls allow most of the classroom community to become observers and benefit from a few children being centered.

A fun variation of the fishbowl leaves one empty chair in the inner circle. The empty chair acts as an invitation for outer-circle members to hop into the circle if they feel like they have a contribution that could also be helpful. This slight shift in the structure can add an extra layer of engagement to the circle.

Sequential Circles
Children add contributions in a clockwise or counterclockwise format.

Nonsequential Circles
Children add contributions as they feel moved to speak.

TYPES OF CIRCLES

Fishbowls
A small group of children contributes to the circle while others watch and listen.

Flexible Fishbowl
A small group of children contributes to the circle. There is one open seat for someone outside the circle to add a contribution.

Open Seat

But Sharing Takes Too Long!

Some of you may be reading about these circle experiences and thinking, "That sounds great, but there is no way this will work in my classroom. It will just take too long!" We hear you. Bringing whole-class circles together can take up quite a bit of time. So here are a few suggestions to help you benefit from circle experiences in time frames that work within our already busy days.

ProTip 1: Give clear expectations about the length of the responses. You might limit some whole-group circles to single-word contributions or short responses. If you think the answer to the circle question will be longer, consider using a fishbowl.

ProTip 2: Break up the class into mini circles of between five and seven children per group. After children have some community circle practice, they learn how to navigate the circle experience, and you can have smaller circles all running at the same time. Children may not hear every voice in the community, but they still benefit from hearing a few different perspectives and ideas from classmates.

ProTip 3: Use small-group circles as another way to personalize learning. To differentiate learning, we might choose questions that fit perfectly for small groups of children and run small-group circles during a reading workshop or while other children are engaged in independent reading.

Bringing Circles to Our Youngest Friends

While trying out this work, we wondered whether circles were a realistic goal for our kindergartners. We asked, "Would 5-year-olds be able to get something truly valuable out of this type of experience?" In the end, the only way to know for sure was to try it out! Here's what we found:

Five-year-olds are capable of amazing things when we scaffold the learning and build slowly. Circles are a new routine to build, so be sure to start off by practicing with fun topics, such as sharing a favorite game or telling the class one thing they do when it snows. We recommend beginning with nonacademic topics for community building in all grades, but as we create this new routine for our primary children, it also serves a dual purpose of learning the rhythms and habits of the routine itself. We can practice the flow of passing the talking piece and using sentence stems to stay focused. We can act as a behind-the-scenes coach, whispering to children as they try out sharing in this way for the first few times.

As we tried reading-based circles with kindergarten friends, we were reminded how important it truly is to return to the book again and again. Not only did the children beg us to bring these books back, rereading and revisiting pages to think in new ways allowed our youngest learners to explore newer, deeper ideas. This close-reading work in kindergarten is all about going back to the familiar with a new purpose: to see new things. Christina Rizzo, a brilliant kindergarten teacher from Paramus, New Jersey, shared that while it did take some time to get circles flowing freely, after practice and a bit of coaching, she was blown away by the things children shared in the circle. Like all good things, the rewards come when we go slowly, offer support, remind children of the expectations and goals, and celebrate each step along the way.

Beyond Circles: Using Prompts for Class Conversations

Sequential and nonsequential circles allow us the gift of every voice. They are beautiful and helpful to our communities in so many ways. They help us learn to listen. They help us slow down and focus on just one thing at a time. They inspire us and bring perspectives to the surface that we might not have considered.

Yet there are times when going around a circle prevents us from getting traction with an idea. Conversations require a back and forth—a pausing, taking in, and readjusting of our own thinking based on the contributions of others. When you seek moments of back and forth, we suggest using the configuration of a circle but offering conversational time for children to grow ideas together, challenge one another, and come to brand-new understandings.

One main difference between conversation circles and more traditional circles is that the goal shifts from collecting voices to using our voices to engage with one another. We begin in a similar fashion—by introducing a question or circle prompt. As children add their contributions, we then invite them to challenge, question, or add on to one another's thoughts. The truth is there isn't a community in existence in which everyone is in constant agreement. This is why we feel that creating a space where children can bring different perspectives to the table and discuss them is vital. And by using the circular shape of our gathering, we remind everyone that the interactions must be done with love and respect.

When Conversations Get Tough

We acknowledge that the goal of flowing, respectful, and easy conversation is a lofty one. We know that whenever people gather around and talk about something powerful, passion can lead us into dangerous territory. After all, we've yet to meet someone who doesn't have some sort of holiday family feud story. Consider yourself lucky if your story doesn't end with Aunt Lucy stomping off, Uncle Tony cursing at everyone, and Grandma looking shocked as she desperately tries to wipe the mashed potatoes out of her hair. We can avoid such scenes, however, if we give children the tools to engage in lively yet lovely conversation.

COMMON SENTENCE STEMS

Some of the lessons in this book offer specific sentence stems to scaffold the sharing of ideas. Here are some common sentence stems for young readers:

- *I think . . .*
- *I wonder . . .*
- *I see . . .*
- *I like . . .*
- *At first . . . but then . . .*
- *I feel like . . .*
- *I think [character] feels . . .*
- *I think [character] is . . .*

One way to keep these circles safe is to use a facilitator. This person reminds us all of the established norms before we enter conversation and then acts as a guide, ensuring that quieter voices are invited to contribute. The facilitator may also pause the conversation, once again reminding the circle of their agreed-upon norms. This creates space for a mindful moment and may simply add a breathing space that can lower the intensity when emotions become heightened. Facilitators are not meant to lead the conversation, nor do they have more power than anyone else. They are simply there to help ensure that we hear one another's voices and maintain respect within our circle.

We can also provide children with tools to help them navigate conversations both in and out of circle experiences. One of our favorite and most impactful tools is using the word *and* in place of *but*. This simple word switch helps us acknowledge someone else's perspective in conversation while adding another idea that may also be true and important to consider. Let's look at an example. Say this sentence aloud: *I understand what you mean, but I think ___.* This wording sends the message that "I hear you, but my perspective is the right one." Now, try this: *I understand what you mean, and I also think that ___. Using and* in place of *but* changes the message to say, "I value your contribution and it deserves to be acknowledged" while also introducing another idea to be considered.

No matter how you choose to bring these conversations forward, we encourage you to embrace disagreement and the challenge of ideas. Sometimes, these conversations will feel uncomfortable, and that is okay. However, if you feel unsure about navigating conversational challenges, try a few of these tools and tips to help you with your journey.

HELPING CHILDREN NAVIGATE CHALLENGING CONVERSATIONS

In her book *Being the Change*, Sara K. Ahmed acknowledges that inviting students into challenging conversations is a must in every classroom and that our learners are going to make mistakes (as are we). This doesn't mean that we should avoid the conversation. Instead, we must teach children how to engage and offer them opportunities to practice. Ahmed writes: "If we want kids to attend to the multiple perspectives around them and listen actively and empathetically, we need to mentor them and show them how" (2018). Check out her book *Being the Change* for invaluable lessons on teaching social comprehension.

How to Grow a Responsive Classroom to Process Difficult Conversations
– Tips from Steve Fiedeldey, International Institute for Restorative Practices (IIRP) Instructor

1. **Plant the seeds of restorative practices early. Feed and nurture deep roots with trust and respect.**
   - Prioritize connection over content.
   - Start with shallow icebreakers, include content-related questions for go-rounds, and eventually lean into more vulnerable, personal questions.
   - Allow student choice in the coursework to demonstrate respect for student autonomy and ownership.

2. Strengthen the network of connection in the classroom forest.

- Just as trees in a forest communicate via an underground network of roots, your classroom will have the same level of interconnectedness when nurtured.
- Use restorative practices to increase responsibility, equity, and empathy.
- Lead and model your own vulnerability. Everyone's story matters, and teachers need to share theirs! When you share your story and lead with vulnerability, children will follow. Together, you will share struggles and joys, allowing for greater insights into one another's perspectives.
- As children share their stories, their roots intertwine around similarities while developing sensitivity to empathy for differences. The strength of this interconnectedness allows for the responsibility and ownership of the class to shift away from the shoulders of the teacher to be shared equally by all learners.

3. When strong winds and difficult conversations come, trust in the strength of the classroom community.

- You are not solely responsible for solving situations or addressing difficult conversations. Lean into the power of the classroom and use the pre-established norms/agreements to remind others of the class's commitments during the healing process.
- Rely on the interconnectedness of your forest. Whether facilitating a difficult conversation or addressing harm that has occurred, true healing comes when an entire community is involved and all voices have a chance to be heard.
- TRUST in your students. Trust in the relationships you have developed together, and trust that their voices and unique lived experiences can heal.
- Hearing from the entire learning community has the greatest potential to effect change.

4. Get comfortable with being uncomfortable.

- You may not have had professional learning, support, or time to prepare prior to a difficult conversation. Do not hesitate to call in others who are further along this learning path to assist in a responsive circle.
- Understanding that a resolution may not be reached is important. Not every difficult conversation ends with a handshake, an understanding of other perspectives, or a hug. Trust in the process. The impact of your collective community may not show itself until weeks or months later, but sometimes we need to give others (and ourselves) the gift of time to grow and change.

Circle Reflection

As you have seen, there's quite a bit of variety in how you can choose to bring circles into your classroom. Regardless of what type of circle you've decided upon, one thing remains the same: Circles should invite reflection. For this reason, we have included an invitation for reflection as a way to close each circle experience. You can do these reflections as another quick circle round, a paired turn-and-talk experience, or simply as a moment of thought.

There are a few common reflection questions that we return to again and again because they get to the heart of why we reflect as a community. Why do we reflect as a community?

- We are one another's teachers and can learn from and be inspired by listening to one another's ideas.
- We find strength in having our ideas affirmed.
- We may see new possibilities or develop new understandings about an alternate point of view when we hear new perspectives.

As the circle closes and the final voices have added their ideas, invite children to stop and think about what they heard from one another during the sharing. As they sit and think, they can use variations of the following questions to help guide their reflection:

- What ideas that were shared stand out to you most?
- What did you hear that taught you something new?
- What new thing can you try?
- What do you now wonder about or want to learn more about?
- What did someone share that made you think, "Me too!"?
- What did someone share that helped you see something in a brand-new way?

Classroom Close-Up: Circles

This Classroom Close-Up offers a glimpse at the structure and flow of conversation within a circle. After sharing a read-aloud, invite children to engage in reflections and discussions that are both deep and meaningful. Circles allow children to come together as a community and share their ideas and perspectives. This is a close-up of a fishbowl-style circle during a lesson with first graders. During their time together, Jigisha shared the story *Alma and How She Got Her Name*, by Juana Martinez-Neal (page 66), and engaged children in the strategies of identity and connection. Following the read-aloud, Jigisha opens the circle by asking children to think about their understanding of the character through Harm and Healing.

Jigisha: Let's think about how Alma felt better from the beginning of the book to the end. What's something that Alma learned that made her happier about her name?

Kate: In the beginning of the story, she looked really sad. And then her dad told her about each of the names she has as part of her name. She learned that each part is from someone in her family, like her grandparents, great-grandparents, and great-aunt. Then she felt special, and by the end of the book she was smiling.

Liam: In the story, Alma felt frustrated and upset about her name. She started feeling happier because she knows that she really liked to draw and so did her grandfather José. That connection made her feel special.

(continued)

Chris: If you look at the pictures on the pages, her smile gets bigger and bigger as you go through the story. *(Chris approaches the front of the class and flips through the pages of the book for his classmates to see.)* It's because she learns what each part of her name means and that she likes the same things as her ancestors.

Miriam: Alma finds something in common with her grandma, like her love for jasmine flowers. Like for me, I am named after my grandma, Mirna, and we are both creative and love baking cupcakes! It makes me happy also when I spend time with my grandma!

Carryover Coaching: Conferring Conversations

We all feel filled up after a powerful class conversation. The community and new ideas grown together are wonderful, and yet for children to achieve continued success, they have to bring their learning and strategies from community time into their independent reading. For true growth, the real goal is transference. In this section, we focus on the Carryover Coaching prompts given for each strategy. Bring these prompts with you into one-on-one conferring conversations and use them to mentor children as they try out new thinking work in their own books.

When to Coach

After teaching a strategy to your whole class and sending children off to cuddle up with their books, you might be tempted to jump right into coaching that particular strategy in your conferences. We sometimes feel the pull of that immediate application, too, and yet we also know that our goal isn't to teach compliance. We want children to apply a strategy as it makes sense in their reading and when it feels like a just-right fit. In other words, the coaching support in each mini-lesson does not need to be an immediate follow-up.

Instead, bring in coaching support as children are ready to apply strategies independently. You might check in by asking lens-based questions to see if or how readers are considering bigger concepts, such as identity or problem/solution. Try some of these prompts and questions as a conversation starter to help you see the kind of coaching a child needs at that time.

Getting to the goal:
- Tell me what you're practicing.
- What are you working on?
- What have you been thinking about?
- What are you trying?

Lens-based starters:
- How have you been thinking about (Identity/Harming & Healing/Heartwork) in your book?
- How are you doing this?
- What have you been paying attention to?

- What has this looked like in your reading?
- Can you show me a place where you've done this?
- Walk me through your thinking.

In addition to the in-the-moment-decision types of conferences, we may also plan some intentional coaching time to support our young readers. These planned interactions often take the form of coaching conferences and small-group support time. We know that mastery doesn't happen in the space of a five-minute conference or a ten-minute mini-lesson. Time and practice are necessary ingredients for growth, and a bit of coaching can assist along the way. If you've already taught a strategy and want to follow up with some one-on-one coaching or if you feel that a small group of learners may benefit from practicing a strategy, you might pull out our Carryover Coaching prompts for small-group practice or reinforcement coaching.

Acknowledging the Balance

Teaching reading in the primary grades is similar to being a server carrying six dishes on one arm and a tray full of drinks on the other arm—while on roller skates! Primary teachers carry a heavy load in being responsible for and trying to balance the teaching of phonemic awareness, phonics, concepts of print, decoding within the context of books, fluency, and reading comprehension— and all in joyful ways that feel exploratory and playful. If no one has explicitly acknowledged that your job is difficult, here it is: Your job is HARD! Starting as primary-grade teachers ourselves, we understand the challenge. And we also remember the joy, the love, and the beauty of each day.

We bring this up because the strategies in this book are tied primarily to one area of teaching reading: comprehension. We know that your time with children isn't solely focused on that. As children learn more and more about how letters and sound work and shift into conventional reading, you need to support their ability to decode the words in their books as well as see that reading is about the message, not just the words on the page. So your conferring is not going to be all about these strategies all the time.

We imagine early primary teachers using the Carryover Coaching slightly differently than teachers who teach later primary. After all, conferring in kindergarten looks a lot different from conferring in second grade. If you're a kindergarten teacher, you might consider using some of our strategies and questions for comprehension conversations during guided reading or other small-group strategy work, as well as quick one-on-one conferences that are focused on the comprehension side of the work. Many of these strategies can be applied even when children are not conventionally reading yet as they explore books and reread texts that they've heard again and again as read-alouds.

In the end, staying balanced is no easy feat. We know that to help our readers grow, we have to do more than teach one thing. Yes, we need to focus on helping them say the words on the page, but our jobs don't end there. We need to teach them that reading is far more than reading the words. Reading is thinking, feeling, learning about the world, wondering, and being inspired. Reading is understanding.

Just Enough

It's tough to find the right balance of support during personalized coaching. We want children to be successful. We want them to laugh at the funny parts and shed a tear with the characters in the sad moments. We want them to understand their books. But we can't let our drive to support them lead us astray. It is very easy for us to lead children, especially when we find them hesitant to chat. However, when our pattern is to lead children, multiple problems follow—from sending messages that there is only one right answer to taking away a child's ability to practice. This is something we must avoid. On the flip side, allowing children to just name a strategy may not be enough. So, if we aren't doing the work for them AND we are not leaving them to do it on their own, what does a coaching conversation sound like?

During coaching conversations, our role is to nudge. We want to slow down the strategy, breaking it into lean prompts that will assist the reader in real time. Like the strategy's steps, prompts begin with actionable verbs, such as *look, read, find*, or *think*. This gives children a tangible step to try out in the moment.

You may notice that the first few times a child tries out a strategy or way of thinking about a book, there will be more pauses and places for you to coach into their process. As children continue practicing, the thinking we might have been coaching them into will become part of their process. Since our goal is ultimately for children to do this work independently, our prompting should fade and we might instead simply offer encouragement and nonverbal cues that reinforce the child's thinking (Goldberg, 2016).

> **LEADING CAN LEAD TO PROBLEMS**
>
> 1. We set up the expectation that children should respond with the idea that is in our mind rather than have a genuine response themselves.
>
> 2. We do all the work, and they know it. Children will pick up on the fact that if they wait a moment or two after you ask a question, you will answer or do the work for them.
>
> 3. Children don't actually practice a skill or strategy at all, so they don't actually grow as a result of our interaction.

Classroom Close-Up: Carryover Coaching Conference

In this Classroom Close-Up, we look at ways we can use our strategies to support children in their independent reading. This is a snapshot of a conference with a second grader. During their time together, Dana asked Noah what he had been working on, listened through asset-based lenses for all of the things he was already doing well, and then used one of the strategies to coach a next step.

A few minutes after their mini-lesson, the children settle in with their book baggies and are soon transported into the worlds of their books. Dana walks over to Noah and asks if she can interrupt his reading for a few minutes to chat. He look up, smiles, and offers her his comfy chair. Thanking him for his gracious offer, Dana slides into another seat next to his desk and leans in to listen, honor, and coach.

Dana: Looks like you're reading one of the Dog Man adventures. *(Noah proudly shows he's on page 101.)* And it looks like you're about halfway through. Awesome! So, let's talk about what you're thinking. We've been studying how we can learn about the characters and their identities, thinking about their challenges and what may hurt them, and trying to really feel with the people in our books. What have you been practicing?

Noah: I've been thinking about the feelings of the characters.

Dana: Cool. Can you share some of that thinking with me? Show me an example from the book. How are you paying attention to their feelings?

Noah: *(Starts flipping through the pages.)* Well, here I knew Dog Man was super excited. *(He points to the picture.)* Look, his eyes are big and his arms are out. *(He points to another section.)* And here he's mad. He wants this. *(Points at the picture.)* And then on this page, he's sad because Petey just yelled at him.

Dana: Oh! It looks like you're looking at different ways you can understand the character's emotions. You're looking at their faces and bodies, you're paying attention to what they want and how it affects them, and you're noticing how the main character feels when they're with other characters. You do all the things we do in real life to understand the emotions of people we're with, and it helps you connect with and understand the main character of your book.

Noah: Yeah. *(Noah looks up and smiles.)*

Dana: I think you're ready to try out another thing around feelings. One other thing that readers do is try to go beyond looking at the main character's feelings and try on the feelings of the other characters to help understand their side of the story. You can do that by looking for an "oh, no" moment between characters. Then, pretend you're one character and look at everything they said and did, and then look at what was said and done to them to feel their feelings. Then, switch places. Pretend to be the other character and push yourself to notice their feelings, too. Think about whether looking at things from the other character's point of view helps you understand what is happening and why it is happening.

Noah: Okay. I'll try that.

Dana: Great! Let me show you. *(Dana opens the book* Joy, *by Corrinne Averiss, a mentor text that the children already know well. She points to the part in the book that shows Fern upset that she wasn't able to bring joy back to her Nanna.)* Remember this part? I'm going to pretend to be Fern. I'm going up to Nanna empty-handed. I couldn't hold any of the joy. I feel disappointed and sad that I couldn't bring joy home for her. Now I'm going to switch places and jump into Nanna's point of view. I see Fern coming toward me with open arms. She tells me how she wanted me to be happy and wanted to bring me joy. This fills up my heart and makes me feel loved and important. Hmm . . . as I think about this part from both characters' points of view, I can understand how they have different feelings. You try.

Noah: *(Opens his book to the last page he was on.)* I'm going to pretend to be Dog Man first.

Dana: Great! As you pretend you're him, think about what you just did. Make the character talk to you.

Noah: *(Takes a moment to close his eyes and imagine himself into the story.)* I just ripped up the bed to put it in the litter box. Petey saw and started yelling at me because of it. I got upset that he was mad at me and yelling.

Dana: Now, switch. Try the other character and look at it from Petey's side.

Noah: I just saw the ripped-up bed in my litter box. Dog Man ruined it, and he's smiling. That makes me so mad. I don't know why he would do that.

Dana: Yes! Now you're looking at feelings from both characters' points of view. That helps you see more about why Petey was yelling. As we read, we can get a fuller picture of the story by pretending we're different characters and understanding their feelings. Keep trying that as you read.

Dana modeling in the book *Joy* while conferring with a second grader

Beyond the Book

The final section in each mentor text invites your class to take the thinking they've done as a community outside of the book and into real-world practice. Our intention is to bridge the literary world with our world and think about how understanding the experiences of real or imagined people from our books can change the way we live every day.

These invitations vary in form. Some of them feature role-play scenarios that allow children to practice how they might act or react in social situations. Others are circle prompts that move away from talking about text and into talking about life. Some prompts are calls to action that invite children to make positive changes in their own communities, while a few are simple mantras that can help us all with the self-talk that leads us in positive directions.

Literacy, Social Comprehension, and SEL

A truth that we often speak is that our job as educators doesn't end with teaching children how to read. Of course we want our students to be able to decode, accumulate text, and think about the books they read once they leave our classrooms. But even more than that, we want to support children in understanding more than just books. We want them to understand themselves, one another, and the world in which they live. We want them to contribute to the communities that they are a part of today and the communities that they will become a part of tomorrow.

Because our goals tie in to supporting reading, social comprehension, and social and emotional learning, many of the lessons and strategies in this book have been inspired by two of our favorite professional communities: Learning for Justice and the Collaborative for Academic, Social, and Emotional Learning (CASEL). If these two organizations are not already bookmarked as favorites on your browser, we suggest you dive into the amazing tools and resources they offer on their sites and through their professional learning opportunities. The lesson work in this book will reference Learning for Justice's Social Justice Standards and CASEL's five areas of competence.

Classroom Close-Up: Beyond-the-Book SEL Connections

The Beyond-the-Book activities that support SEL offer a variety of formats—from games and circles to self-regulatory breathing exercises. It takes a mixture of practice, reflection, community, and strategy to help ourselves grow our emotional wellness and connection with others, hence, the variety. However, the fact that these experiences vary so much made it hard to decide which lesson to offer as a fly-on-the-wall experience. After some reflection and conversation, the choice became crystal clear: We needed to center the vocabulary lesson.

We imagine many of you just did the "Wait... What???" double-take. "What does vocabulary have to do with SEL?" you may ask. Our answer: Everything.

(continued)

In her book *All About Love*, author bell hooks teaches us: "Definitions are vital starting points for the imagination. What we cannot imagine cannot come into being" (2018). If we don't deeply understand the definitions of *love, compassion,* and *generosity,* how do we move ourselves into action with love? If we cannot recognize our own emotions, how do we regulate and move forward? (Bracket, 2020) Regulation and connection start with accurately defining and recognizing emotion. And yet most people—children and adults alike—narrowly describe emotions in three simple words: *happy, sad, mad* (Brown, 2022). And so, we must start by teaching the vocabulary of the heart and develop co-authored definitions of our emotions together. We recommend making this emotion-defining work a repeated practice so that children have the necessary language as they step into the work of practicing empathy and recognizing their own heart space.

After reading the story *Best Day Ever!*, by Marilyn Singer (page 74), and hearing many children consistently use the word *sad* to describe the little boy's emotions after yelling at his dog, Dana decided to bring a new heart word into the mix: the word *guilty*. In the interaction below, children explore the word *guilty*, connecting that emotion to the story and developing their own visuals and language to bring clarity to this new feeling word. Dana gathers the children together onto the carpet with the book, a piece of chart paper, and some markers in hand.

Dana: Hi, Friends! The last time we visited, I read you the story *Best Day Ever!*, and we pretended our way through the book, looking at how all of the characters felt. We saw lots of ups and downs as we moved through the story, and we said that there were happy moments and sad moments. But we also know that there are different kinds of happy and different kinds of sad. Today, we are going to try out a new word that describes a kind of sad. The word is *guilty*. Thumbs up if you've heard this word before. *(Children show a mix of thumbs up, thumbs in the middle, and thumbs down.)* It sounds like this word is familiar to some of us and newer to others. Let's word explore!

Dana writes the word *guilty* on chart paper and invites children to say the word with her as she runs her finger under the letters. She gives a child-friendly definition and connects the feeling to the book.

Dana: To me, feeling guilty happens when I know I did something wrong or something that hurt someone else and I'm a little sad for them and mad at myself. It feels sad/mad. Let's find a guilty spot in the book. *(Dana turns to the page in* Best Day Ever! *that shows the boy looking at the puppy curled up under the table.)* Hmm . . . In this part, the boy just yelled at his puppy for knocking down the lamp, but then he saw how he made the puppy upset and scared. Let's look closely at the picture and see what the boy's guilty body and face look like. What do you notice? Turn and talk to your partner.

Dana listens in and hears responses, such as "His face looks sad" and "His lips are down." After a moment, she brings the children back together.

Dana: We noticed a lot about the boy's face. Let's remember that look. Now, I'm going to try to remember a guilty moment from my own life. Hmm . . . Let me think. I know! I remember one time that I felt guilty. Last week I was looking all over the house for one of my favorite books. I remembered that my son John was reading it a few days before, so I asked him where he put it. He swore he gave it back to me, but I didn't believe him and told him that he couldn't use my things if he'd lose them. It just wasn't responsible. I was mad at him and made him feel bad. Then, later that night, I was looking in my bag and found the book. He did give it back, and I forgot. I yelled at him and made him feel bad, but it was really my fault. I had that sad-for-hurting-him-and-mad-at-myself feeling called *guilty*. Now, you try to think of a guilty-feeling story from your life when you had that sad-for-hurting-someone-or-doing-something-wrong-and-mad-at-yourself feeling. It might sound like this: "One time I . . ." or "I felt guilty when . . ." Turn and talk to share your story.

The children turn to one another and share stories about not letting a friend join a game, pushing a sister, taking a toy from someone else, and so on. Dana invites children to bring the feeling back and use their bodies to show it.

Dana: Let's remember what our guilty feelings looked like on our bodies. Let's show guilty with our faces. And now with our bodies. Look around. What do you notice about what guilty looks like? Turn and talk.

Dana uses the descriptions children name to make a sketch of what guilty looks like under the word on the chart. To end the lesson, she invites all the children to say what guilty means in their own words in a final turn and talk. Here are two sweet samples of first-grade definitions of *guilty:*

"When you hurt someone and your heart needs a band-aid." —Samantha

"A heavy, mucky feeling because you feel bad for doing something wrong." —Tommy

Dana: Wow, we really understand the feeling guilty now, don't we? Let's remember that when we notice the feeling of sad/mad after we've done something wrong or a sad/mad feeling from a character after they've done something wrong, we can use the word *guilty* to name that feeling.

Reading Aloud and Revisiting Stories

The mentor texts featured in this book are not meant to be one-and-done reading experiences. Introduce a chosen text to children as an engaging read-aloud. During this initial visit, children follow characters through the twists and turns of the plot and pause to react to the characters' experiences and emotions. Choose multiple stopping points along the way to share your own thoughts and invite children to think about the story.

Let's take a moment to explore the two types of read-aloud experiences: **read-aloud** and **interactive read-aloud**. When some of us think about read-aloud time, we imagine children huddled together listening to the teacher read a story straight through without interruption. These community moments offer children an opportunity to hear a book come to life with fluent and expressive reading and to simply enjoy a story together. These types of read-alouds are certainly worthy of our class time. However, read-alouds can also take on an instructional lens. In the interactive read-aloud experience, the reader pauses at chosen points to model some thinking or to invite children to consider new ideas and put some strategies into practice (Fountas & Pinnell, 2001).

There is no right or wrong read-aloud practice when you engage in a first read. Follow your heart and feel free to mix it up. Either way, before diving into explicit strategy work or circle practice, children should first experience the book as a joyful community read. As Maria Walther shares in her wonderful book *The Ramped-Up Read Aloud,* "A read aloud should be a joyful celebration for all. For you, for your students, and indirectly, for the author and illustrator who toiled over each word and every image that lies on and between the covers of the book" (2019).

After the classroom community has enjoyed the story together, that book becomes a mentor text that can be revisited again and again for different purposes. It is during these revisits that you will highlight specific parts to model a **strategy**, invite a **circle** conversation, or tap into a **beyond-the-book** social and emotional learning experience. Each mini-lesson features a preselected section of the book for you to revisit and explicitly teach the strategy. In these moments, we reread a short section of text and model for children how we think through the chosen strategy so we can offer them a clear example of the strategy in action. Think about your revisit decisions as an if-then scenario. If you want to teach a clear strategy for a way readers think about texts, then revisit with a mini-lesson. If you want to offer a space for perspective sharing and benefiting from one another's ideas, then revisit with a circle. And if you want to use the text as a catalyst for some social comprehension work, then revisit with a beyond-the-book lesson.

READ ALOUD

Enjoy the book as a class community. Pause at times to think aloud and invite children's thoughts and reactions.

REVISIT FOR MINI-LESSON

Look back on a small section. Use that section to model your thinking through a strategy.

REVISIT FOR CIRCLE

Share the circle question with children. Reread a portion of the text or the whole story before the circle chat.

REVISIT FOR SEL

Revisit sections of the book that highlight lessons, role-playing, or other social and emotional learning activities.

Classroom Close-Up: 1st Grade Read-Aloud

Interactive read-aloud is a favorite time in most classrooms. There is something magical about gathering around a story. Storytelling is an ancient tradition, so maybe stories are part of our very DNA. Or perhaps it is simply that when we gather around for a story, we feel connected and can get lost in a new time and space. Whatever the reasons, for us read-aloud time is pure joy.

In this read-aloud experience, we invite children to step into the world of different characters to get a fuller picture of the whole story. Multiple pausing points allow children to listen and then practice the art of stepping into another's place. The way it begins . . . We gather.

Clutching the book *Best Day Ever!,* by Marilyn Singer, to her chest, Dana invites all of her first-grade friends to the classroom carpet to sit with their partners. When everyone has settled into their special spot on the rug and Dana is seated in the rocking chair, we are ready.

Dana: Hello, Readers! It looks like we're all ready to settle in for a very special story. Today, I brought a favorite of mine about a little puppy and his owner. In this story, we get to follow them through a whole day together to see what kinds of adventures come their way. Today as we read, we are also going to do one of our favorite things: pretend the story. This time, as we go, let's pretend our way into both characters' hearts and minds. This is important because even when the same thing is happening, different characters can be thinking and feeling different things. To really understand the whole story, we want to see things through the eyes of both characters.

Dana holds the book up for all the children to see, reads the cover, and asks children for their first impressions. Based on the cover, she invites them to share one thing they expect characters to feel with their turn-and-talk partners. She listens in while they quickly chat. After sharing a few thoughts from the children, Dana begins to read the story.

Dana pauses reading on a page at the beginning that shows the boy and the puppy first thing in the morning and models pretending. She uses her body to act and voices aloud the things she's thinking and feeling as the characters.

Dana: I'm going to pause here and do some pretending. First, let me pretend to be the dog. *Jump up on my boy. Lick, lick, lick. I'm so happy to see him this morning. I'm feeling great.* Now, I'm going to swap and pretend to be the boy. *Eyes open, and there's my dog! Hi, puppy. Thanks for the licks. I'm happy to see you, too!*

Dana reads on, inviting children to say the repeating line of "best day ever" with her as she goes. She pauses again at the part in which the puppy chases the snake in the lake. On this page, she invites children to think about what is happening, using both the words she read and the picture for reference. Then, she lets the children try out the pretending.

Dana: Let's pretend to be the puppy first. *Swim, swim, swim, get that snake.* Look closely at the picture. Think like a puppy. How are you feeling? Why? Turn and talk to tell your partners.

The students chatter while Dana listens and coaches.

Dana: Okay, now let's switch! Pretend you're the little boy at the dock watching your puppy. Use the picture to help you pretend. What are you calling out? What are you thinking and feeling? Pretend with your partners, and then share what you feel.

Dana goes back to listen and coach. After a moment, she brings the children back together and shares a few of their ideas.

Dana: I heard some of you talking about how scary it felt to see the puppy chasing the snake, and other people talked about being worried. Wow! Even though we're on the same page, the characters we pretended to be have very different feelings. The boy knows how dangerous a snake can be, but the puppy doesn't. Let's keep going.

Dana reads on again and pauses briefly to pretend to be the puppy when the boy pushes her off his lap. She shares that she's sad and confused about him not wanting her licks this time. Then, Dana continues to read until the page in which the puppy knocks down the lamp. This is another opportunity for paired pretending. Using the partner names of "Peanut Butter and Jelly," Dana gives the children different roles for this part of the story.

Dana: This time let's partner pretend. Peanut Butter partner, you pretend to be the boy. Jelly partner, you pretend to be the dog. Turn and pretend.

The children jump right into their character's role and pretend. There is yelling and pouty faces all around the room. In the midst of this, Dana pauses them and asks them to name how the different characters felt and why. Then she reinforces their ideas.

Dana: You all noticed that the boy was angry. There was a big mess, and he was mad at the puppy. But she felt very different. She knew she made a mistake, and she was feeling scared and sad because her boy was yelling at her.

Dana reads on until the last page. She invites children to jump into one more pretend play as the boy says he's sorry. This time, instead of turning to chat, she has them pretend to be both the boy and then the puppy.

(continued)

Dana: What do you think this time? Are the feelings the same or different? Thumbs up for the same and thumbs down for different. Ah . . . I see lots of the same. Okay, so what feeling word would you use to say how they feel at the end? Tell me on the count of three.

As she puts the book on the easel, Dana shares how pretending to be different characters helps us notice how even when characters are in the same part of the book together, they can experience things very differently. She sends air high fives across to everyone and reminds them that as they read, they can do this pretending, too.

Jigisha reading aloud to first graders

THE LESSONS PART

"Reading is not walking on the words; it's grasping the soul of them."

– Paulo Freire

We wrote a book focused on mentor texts because we believe the characters, images, and words on the pages of a book can touch our souls and shape the people we become. Books can offer children learning opportunities well beyond skill development and enjoyment. Books hold our humanity, and reading about the lives of real or imagined characters can give children the gift of understanding themselves and one another.

Lesson Page Close Up

Each lesson begins with a mini exploration of the mentor text that includes a genre description, grade-level recommendation, and a summary of the book. You'll also find three lessons—one for each Reading Lens—that offer strategies with places to pause and model your thinking process, questions that can be used for whole-class conversations and circles, and carryover coaching prompts that bring these ways of thinking into small groups and conferring work.

#OwnVoices Indicates that the book's author and/or illustrator shares the identity of the main character.

A Bit About the Book Gives some information about the featured mentor text. Along with the book's title, this section provides a summary of its content and message.

Lesson Provides a step-by-step process for teaching a skill.

Places to Pause Suggests pages in the book where teachers can model their thinking.

Circle Questions Offers questions for literacy circles and whole-class comprehension conversations.

Skills and Standards Names the comprehension skills, Common Core standards, Social Justice standards, and CASEL connections addressed in each lesson. Our goal is to marry social and reading comprehension in our conversations about books.

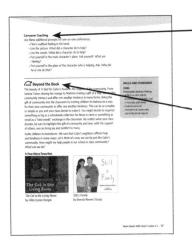

Carryover Coaching Provides general questions and prompts teachers can use to bring the strategy to independent readers in reading conferences.

Beyond the Book Extends the work into intentional SEL study using games, self-regulation strategies, or community projects. Each activity is designed to help children build community and practice social comprehension.

Note: Italicized phrasing and questions offer examples of verbiage and questions you can use in the classroom. Our intention is not to create a script but to share sample language.

We wish we could include all the books we have read and loved and tell all our stories within this text. However, we are limited to page numbers that help make this book a little lighter to carry in our classrooms. At the end of the lesson pages, you will find a few more book recommendations that invite us all to continue deeply exploring the lives of people, identities, homes, and worlds.

Putting Lessons Into Practice

Anything worth deep study deserves more than a one-time visit. We imagine the concepts of Identity, Harm and Healing, and Heartwork are threads that weave across the school year. Each woven lesson provides yet another stitch in the blanket of literacy and social-emotional learning.

The lessons on the following pages are designed to fit within any literacy framework or program. To be clear, this resource is not intended to become a whole program or curriculum. We see this book as a tool to enhance your yearlong study, not replace it. There are countless ways you can bring these stories, conversations, and strategies into your classroom study, and we trust that you will find your own unique approach to incorporate the work. We invite you to consider a few possibilities for adding or swapping out some of the books you are currently using for those in this section.

Here are a few suggested frameworks for choosing lessons:
- Matching skills and standards
- Matching genres
- Connecting to content areas
- Honoring celebrations, identities, and relationships

Matching Skills and Standards

As with most large shifts in education, the adoption of the Common Core State Standards in 2010 was anything but smooth sailing. Dana remembers many a faculty meeting spent sitting around a table with her first-grade teacher colleagues, and everyone scratching their heads trying to figure out what these new standards meant and how they would change the work they were doing with their students. They debated, looked at student samples through the lenses of the standards, and spoke at length about the developmental appropriateness of certain ideas. Coming to their own interpretations of the meaning behind the standards took time and energy. Many struggled with concepts such as text-dependent questions and finding authentic and meaningful ways to bring close reading into a first-grade classroom. It certainly wasn't all fun and games, and many of the practices they tried were abandoned. Yet in the end, the team found value in the way these standards worked as a giant learning progression—laying out a K–12 view of how skills grew with study and practice. In addition, the standards gave more clarity to the importance of focusing on different genres and balancing fiction and nonfiction reading experiences. Most important, the layers of comprehension standards sent the message that literacy learning was about making meaning and not simply about learning letter-sound correspondence and decoding words on the page.

It's been more than a decade since Common Core came into being, and in that time, the lessons we've learned through implementation have led many states to revise or create their own versions of the standards. This is how learning goes—we try something new, we reflect, we celebrate our successes, we learn from our failures, we refine. Today, standards are just one tool to help us plan our literacy lessons. We know there is no magic wand that will accelerate growth, but we can hold up the standards as a way to consider some important frames and skills that will help children explore texts and their ideas about those texts in new and interesting ways.

If your lesson planning is centered around different standards or skills, you can use the book chart online (see page 6 for how to access) to match the standard/skill you are teaching with our books and lessons that address that type of learning. For example, if you need books and lessons that support standard RL.1.3 *(Describe characters, settings, and major events in a story, using key details)*, you can scan the book chart and find texts with lessons that address that standard (see example on the following page).

Title	Author/ Illustrator	Identities represented*	Ideas represented	Genre	Core standards	Identity	Harm and Healing	Heartwork	Awards
Alma and How She Got Her Name	Juana Martinez-Neal	Ethnicity: Latine; Culture: Peruvian	Name story	Realistic fiction	RL.K.1, RL.K.3, RL.K.7; SL.K.1.A–B, SL.K.2, SL.K.6; RL.1.1, RL.1.3, RL.1.7; SL.1.1.A, SL.1.2, SL.1.6	Readers explore the identities of characters by paying close attention to what the characters love and do.	Readers look for problems and ways that make the character feel better or fix the problem.	Readers feel the characters' feelings by paying close attention to those characters' faces.	2019 Caldecott Honor Book; Ezra Jack Keats Book Award

* Like all of us, the characters and subjects in books carry multiple identities. Our identities go beyond our cultural heritage and races. Identities are also our family roles, our careers, our interests, and so much more. It would be impossible to capture every part of a character's identities in a small chart; therefore, we focus on only a few for each book. The list shown here does not capture a full picture of someone's identity.

Matching Genres

In addition to focusing on skills and standards, many educators organize learning through genre studies. There may be times in the year when we invite children to read primarily biography texts, or we may take a dip into folklore or historical fiction. These genre studies give children the opportunity to explore elements and specific characteristics tied to different text types and broaden the ways they create meaning. When planning for genre studies, you might decide to focus on the genre category on our book chart online. Then, scan and select texts that would support the genre exploration that you and your students are about to engage in.

Connecting to Content Areas

While it is true that the focus of the strategies and circle conversations in this book are connected primarily to literacy, the stories we've chosen may also find their way into content-area teaching. Dana, Keisha, and Jigisha have always found that the most authentic and engaging ways to learn content are through play, curiosity, and storytelling. Bringing picture books into the content areas can ignite interest and invite children to bring their most curious selves into that study. A picture book can be just the tool that you need, whether to introduce a new topic or to connect abstract concepts to real-life experiences and people. Check out the book chart online for matches to people, time periods, and even scientific discoveries that fit with the content you are teaching. These books and lessons may be a way to bring a bit more storytelling and context to subjects you're studying in history and science.

Honoring Celebrations, Identities, and Relationships

Lastly, we'd like to honor that not all learning fits into neat categories, such as reading instruction, math, or science. Sometimes, our learning is inspired by celebrating the wonderful people in our lives and in our world. While we don't need to—nor should we—follow a calendar to bring different cultures into our classroom, books are a wonderful kickoff to honor cultural celebrations, such as Hispanic Heritage Month or Grandparents Day. We do not suggest sorting the identities represented in our highlighted texts into categories, such as Pride Month books, Black History Month books, and so on. We strongly believe that representation of all different identities should be woven across time. However, you might see that one of the titles listed in this book provides an ideal opening into a celebration.

In our role as educators, we have opportunities to dedicate ourselves to transforming our teaching by celebrating this work throughout the year—and not just in a particular month. The stories found within this book offer an invitation and an opportunity to dive deeper into these lessons! If one way to use these texts is as an entry point into a cultural celebration, you can use the identities section of our book chart online to match up the people that you may be honoring with great biographies and books. You may circle back to the same text at another time of the year to offer a lesson through Harm and Healing, and again in another moment, through Heartwork. The flexibility of the lessons found within this section offers educators numerous options and provides children with multiple experiences with one text.

As you move into the lessons on the following pages, we hope you will see the beauty both in the texts and in the conversation and thinking that we invite children to engage in with one another. We hope these conversations in classrooms will help children feel seen, appreciated, and inspired. We hope you will feel that way as well.

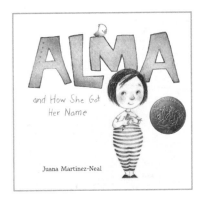

ALMA AND HOW SHE GOT HER NAME

Written and illustrated by Juana Martinez-Neal
Grades K–1 / Fiction / #OwnVoices

A Bit About the Book

This story of self-exploration brings readers on an emotional joyride. Each page lifts us as Alma Sofia Esperanza José Pura Candela, who at first is not so happy with her long name, learns the history of how each name was chosen. Her many names connect her with her family's history, and we watch her find herself in each of the people she's named after. This story celebrates tradition and family connection, as well as the importance of bringing our own authentic selves to the world. **Note:** This book is available both in Spanish and English. You may want to acquire both for your library.

SKILLS AND STANDARDS

Comprehension Skill:
Infer about character

CCSS: RL.K.3, RL.K.7 • SL.K.1.A–B, SL.K.2, SL.K.6 • RL.1.3, RL.1.7 • SL.1.1.A, SL.1.2, SL.1.6

Social Justice:
ID.K-2.1 (I know and like who I am and can talk about my family and myself and name some of my group identities.)

CASEL:
Social Awareness
• Demonstrate empathy and compassion
• Show concern for the feelings of others

Identity

Strategy: Readers explore the identities of characters by paying close attention to what the characters love and do.

As You Read . . .

• Zoom in on a character.
• Look closely at the words and the pictures to notice what the character enjoys and does on the pages.
• List the things the character enjoys.

Places to Pause

Pause on the page that features the words "I am Sofia." Using the words and pictures, point out Alma and her grandmother's shared love of flowers and books. Tell children that what we enjoy is clearly part of our identities, so as we notice what both Sofia and Alma love, we learn about who they are.

Circle Questions

Say to children: *Think about all the things Alma and her family members enjoy and spend their time doing. What do we learn about Alma's identity?* Consider making a predictable chart from children's contributions. You might use sentence stems, such as: "Alma is . . ." or "Alma loves to . . ."

On sticky notes, children drew sketches to show what they learned about Alma's identity through the things she loves.

Afterwards, invite children to reflect by asking: *What did someone share that helped you see something brand new about Alma that you didn't notice before?*

Carryover Coaching

Use these additional prompts for one-on-one conferences.

- Look closely at the page.
- Look for smiles. Notice what the character is doing there.
- Ask yourself: *What am I learning about that character?*

Harm and Healing

Strategy: Readers look for problems and ways that make the character feel better or fix the problem.

As You Read . . .

- Name the problem.
- Look for a part that shows the character feeling better.
- Ask: *What did the character do or learn that helped her feel better?*

Places to Pause

Pause on the page in which Alma says, "I love the story of my name!" As you model your thinking, refer back to the beginning of the book when Alma felt unhappy about having such a long name. Compare the way she looks on that page to the way she looks on this page and her exclamation about loving her name. Think aloud about how learning about her family members changed the way Alma felt and fixed her problem.

Circle Questions

Say to children: *Let's think about how Alma's feelings changed from the beginning of the book to the end. What's something that Alma learned that made her happier about her name?*

Afterwards, invite children to reflect by asking: *What did someone share that you also thought about already? What did someone share that you had not thought of yet?*

Carryover Coaching

Use these additional prompts for one-on-one conferences.

- Find a place where the character feels better.
- Look for what changed. What's happening?
- Name what fixed the problem.

Heartwork

Strategy: Readers feel the characters' feelings by paying close attention to those characters' faces.

As You Read . . .
• Zoom in on the character's face.
• Look at the character's mouth, eyes, and cheeks.
• Ask: *How can you tell from the character's face how he or she feels?*
• Copy the character's expression on your own face. For example, if the character's eyes are closed, close your eyes, too. Feel the character's feeling in your heart, too.

Places to Pause
Pause on the page that shows Alma lighting the candle. Model your thinking by describing Alma's closed eyes, round cheeks, and closed-mouth smile. Show children how you can make your face match Alma's face, and then describe the feeling of joy and love that you feel.

Circle Questions
Say to children: *We can all feel Alma's changing feelings across the book. Pick a page in which you felt a big feeling along with the character. Tell us the part and the big feeling in your heart. Say why you felt that way.* Offer this sentence stem to support the sharing: "When Alma . . . I felt . . . because . . ."

Afterwards, invite children to reflect by asking: *What did someone share that made you think, "Me, too"?*

Carryover Coaching
Use these additional prompts for one-on-one conferences.
• Look closely at a character's face.
• Think about how her face matches what is happening.
• Notice her mouth, eyes, and so on.
• Name her feeling.
• Try on that face and feeling, too.

 **Beyond the Book**

Celebrate the names and identities of the children in your class. Invite children to write or decorate their own names with colors and pictures that express things they love. You might also bring your caregiver community into the activity by sending home a note inviting them to tell their child the story of how their name was chosen. Then, have a name party! Encourage children to share their name pictures by describing their illustrations or telling the story of their names.

SKILLS AND STANDARDS

CASEL:
Self-Awareness
• Integrate personal and social identities
• Identify personal, cultural, and linguistic assets

A Few More Favorites

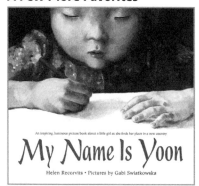

My Name Is Yoon
by Helen Recorvits

That's Not My Name
by Anoosha Syed

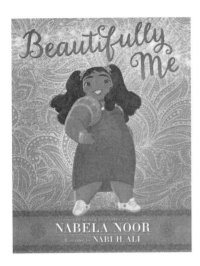

BEAUTIFULLY ME

Written by Nabela Noor / Illustrated by Nabi H. Ali

Grade 2 / Fiction / #OwnVoices

A Bit About The Book

Beautifully Me illustrates the importance of developing an understanding of beauty that goes beyond the body. The story focuses on Zubi Chowdhury, whose joy about attending her first day of school is challenged by the messages she receives from others about body size. From the beginning of the story, she observes characters' responses to their own or another's body size. The beliefs their words and actions convey about beauty impact the way she thinks about herself. With the help of her family, Zubi learns beauty is not defined by body size and comes to accept and love herself.

SKILLS AND STANDARDS

Comprehension Skill:
Infer about character

CCSS: RL.2.1, RL.2.3, RL.2.5, RL.2.6 • SL.2.1.B, SL.2.3, SL.2.4

Social Justice:
ID.K-2.1 (I know and like who I am and can talk about my family and myself and name some of my group identities.)

CASEL:
Self-Awareness
• Examine prejudices and biases
Social Awareness
• Identify diverse social norms, including unjust ones
Responsible Decision-Making
• Demonstrate curiosity and open-mindedness

 Identity

Strategy: Readers learn that other characters' thoughts, actions, and words can affect the way the main character thinks, acts, or speaks about herself.

As You Read . . .

- Notice the main character as she hears and sees what the other characters say and do.
- Look at the thoughts or questions the main character has in response to what she hears or sees.
- Ask: *How do these help me understand about the effect the other characters have on the main character?*

Places to Pause

Focus on the ways Zubi learns how her mother, sister, father, and classmate feel about body size. Share about how their thinking affects Zubi's view of herself. Pause on the pages in which the characters say:

- "Look at this tummy. I'm getting too big."
- "I'm on a diet. I want to lose weight so I can look pretty in time for the school dance."
- Baba laughed and patted his belly. "I put on some pounds. Ma, I am up to a large now. Not good."
- "Alix, you look fat in that dress."

Circle Questions

The ways another person treats or speaks to him- or herself or to someone else can affect what we believe about ourselves. Ask children: *What beliefs about body size does Zubi begin to learn from her mother, father, sister, and classmate based on what they say or do?*

Afterwards, invite children to reflect by saying: *Listen to your classmates' thinking. Consider how you can add on to what they say by sharing actions or words from the story.*

Carryover Coaching

Use these additional prompts for one-on-one conferences.

- Look closely at the statement each character makes about him- or herself or about another character and any related actions.
- Think about what their words and related actions say about their beliefs or thoughts.
- Say something about each character's beliefs: *Based on the book, I think* (character) *believes that a bigger body type is . . . I say this because . . .*

Second graders share evidence from the book for what they believe characters think about body sizes.

 Harm and Healing

Strategy: Readers learn that differences in the points of view of the characters in the story can help identify the problem.

As You Read . . .

- Notice the point in the story in which the main character's point of view is most clear.
- Determine if the main character's point of view is the same as or different than that of the other characters.
- Identify the words, actions, or thoughts of the other characters that support your decision.
- Share your thoughts: *I believe* (the main character) *thinks the same/ different things than* (another character). *The part of the text that helps me know this is . . .*

Places to Pause

Pause on the two pages in which Zubi tells her family the messages she learned about beauty and body size throughout the day. Reread the pages. Think aloud: *None of these words or actions were directed at Zubi, but she is still sad. She even says, "I don't want kids to make fun of me, too!" I think that means she is putting herself in the place of others and actually feels the unkind words."*

Next, pause on the page in which Baba and Zubi are the only characters pictured in Zubi's room. Slowly walk through the next three pages, pointing to the things each minor character says to help Zubi understand other people's points of view.

SKILLS AND STANDARDS

Comprehension Skill: Distinguish characters' points of view

CCSS: RL.2.1, RL.2.3, RL.2.5, RL.2.6 • SL.2.1C, SL.2.3, SL.2.4, SL.2.6

Social Justice: JU.K-2.12 (I know when people are treated unfairly.)

CASEL: Social Awareness
- Demonstrate empathy and compassion
- Take others' perspectives
- Identify diverse social norms, including unjust ones

Relationship Skills
- Seek or offer support and help when needed

Circle Questions

Say to children: *Sometimes, the hurt we witness is too difficult for us to deal with by ourselves. In the story, Zubi struggles to understand why people can be mean to themselves or to others because of body size. The feelings become too much for her to handle by herself. How have others' reflection of their points of view help Zubi fully understand what she believes about body size?*

Afterwards, invite children to reflect by saying: *Think about what your classmates said. What is another thing from the story that you can add to support their statements?*

Carryover Coaching

Use these additional prompts for one-on-one conferences.

- Look for parts of the story that tell what the main character thinks or believes.
- Look for parts that tell what other characters think or believe.
- Ask: *Are there any thoughts or beliefs that are the same or different for more than one character? Do these similarities or differences help me understand the problem in the story?*

SKILLS AND STANDARDS

Comprehension Skill:
Infer about character

CCSS: RL.2.3, RL.2.6 • SL.2.1A, SL.2.3, SL.2.4, SL.2.6

Social Justice:
- AC.K-2.18 (I will say something or tell an adult if someone is being hurtful, and will do my part to be kind even if I don't like something they say or do.)
- AC.K-2.20 (I will join with classmates to make our classroom fair for everyone.)

CASEL:
Social Awareness
- Demonstrate empathy and compassion
- Show concern for the feelings of others
- Take others' perspectives
Relationship Skills
- Practice teamwork and collaborative problem-solving
- Resolve conflicts constructively

Heartwork

Strategy: Readers can use words and illustrations in a story to learn about societal norms and determine if they are fair.

As You Read . . .

- Determine if the problem in the story happens only in the book or if it is something that happens in the world beyond the text.
- Look for a part in which the illustration and the text show how a character feels about the problem in the story.
- Ask: *Does the character think the problem represents something that is fair or unfair?*

Places to Pause

Pause on the pages that show Amma and Baba talking with Zubi about her name. Point to Zubi's eyes and comment aloud about the emotions she must be feeling. Read the words Zubi says: "I don't even know what 'beautiful' means anymore."

Circle Questions

Read the page on which Zubi says her name and affirms who she is. Ask children: *Have you ever questioned something you had thought of as beautiful because of thoughts or beliefs that others shared about it? Did this questioning change your belief? In what way?*

Afterwards, invite children to reflect by saying: *Think about what your classmates shared. What new ideas did they share that you might be able to use when other people's thoughts, words, or actions cause you to question what you believe?*

Carryover Coaching
Use these additional prompts for one-on-one conferences.
- Find an idea, like a stereotype, that some people in the real world believe.
- Consider if believing in this idea is fair or if it causes harm.

Beyond the Book

This book teaches some powerful lessons about point of view—a requirement for empathy—and mindfulness. As we journey with Zubi on her first day of school, we watch her quietly observe and try to make sense of other people's negative messages about bigger bodies. Through questioning—instead of just accepting—others' beliefs, Zubi shows us the value of being curious about things that people do or say as well as the importance of considering the outcomes of different perspectives. As her family comes together to help her work through the emotional challenges of the day, we learn to be mindful of the ways we can harm ourselves and those who love us without meaning to do so. To be more mindful of others in the moments when our thoughts turn negative, we can follow Zubi's example: observe, question, and consider how the actions we see done to others or the words we hear said about others make us feel.

Say to children: *After hearing Kennedy say something unkind about Alix and seeing her laugh, Zubi questions whether the things she has observed are true and kind. How can we do this questioning when we are on the playground? What do we think friends (like Alix) who receive these types of unkind words or actions would want us to do to demonstrate our empathy toward them?*

SKILLS AND STANDARDS

CASEL
Responsible Decision-Making
- Demonstrate curiosity and open-mindedness
- Learn to make a reasoned judgment after analyzing information, data, facts

A Few More Favorites

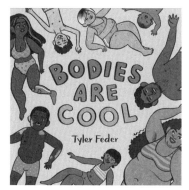

Bodies Are Cool
by Tyler Feder

I Am Enough
by Grace Byers

BEST DAY EVER!

Written by Marilyn Singer / Illustrated by Leah Nixon
Grades K–1 / Fiction / #OwnVoices

A Bit About the Book

This book invites us into the mind and heart of an energetic and loving puppy as we follow her through the day. In true puppy fashion, the day has moments of happiness and fun, as well as moments when she finds herself in a bit of trouble. From the pure joy of digging in the garden and chasing kitties up a tree to prancing in mud and cuddling up with a stinky fish, the puppy finds herself on a rollercoaster ride of feelings. This story invites readers to sort through the sadness of mistakes and the beauty of forgiveness.

SKILLS AND STANDARDS

Comprehension Skill:
Infer about character

CCSS: RL.K.2, RL.K.3, RL.K.7 • SL.K.1.A–B, SL.K.2, SL.K.5, SL.K.6 • RL.1.2, RL.1.3, RL.1.7 • SL.1.1.A, SL.1.2, SL.1.5, SL.1.6

Social Justice:
DI.K-2.10 (I find it interesting that groups of people believe different things and live their daily lives in different ways.)

CASEL:
Social Awareness
• Recognize strengths in others

Identity

Strategy: Readers use pictures of characters to learn more about their identity.

As You Read . . .

- Look closely at the pictures.
- Ask: *What am I learning about this character from the picture?*
- List what you've learned.

Places to Pause

Pause on the page that shows the puppy passing the little boy a sock. Share that you want to study the picture to learn more about the character. Point to parts of the picture that reveal different aspects of the character. You might say something like: *I see the character is a child. The character seems to be a boy. I notice that this boy uses a wheelchair to move around.* Afterwards, pause to reflect on how much you have learned just by looking at the picture and briefly list the things you pointed out again for children.

Circle Questions

For this circle, we will step out of the book to explore different parts of identity. Choose a few images of people, such as photos of familiar friends or maybe a few stock photos. Be sure to select photos that show diverse representations of people. Then, invite children to study a photo closely and choose a word that tells one part of the person's identity. Say: *Let's all look closely at the photo. Notice a few different things that we can learn about the person by studying the picture. Then, choose just one word to share in the circle. We'll listen to everyone and collect the different words we choose to share.*

Afterwards, invite children to reflect by saying: *Think about everything our classmates noticed. Think about how you may be able to understand more about people by noticing different parts of their identity that tell who they are.*

Carryover Coaching
Use these additional prompts for one-on-one conferences.
- Point to one of the characters in the picture.
- Move your finger over the character's different parts and name what you see.

Harm and Healing

Strategy: Readers know that problems have two parts—an outside part (what happened) and a heart part (how what happened made a character feel).

As You Read . . .
- Notice when a character has a problem.
- Think aloud: *What happened? What went wrong?*
- Ask: *How did what happened make the character feel?*

Places to Pause
Pause on the page that shows the puppy jumping onto the boy's lap. Think aloud about what happened—the outside problem. *(The dog was dirty and smelly, and the little boy didn't want to be close to her.)* Then, share how what happened only tells us part of the story. The feelings caused by what happened are just as important. Talk to children about the boy's anger and how it made the puppy feel scared and sad.

Circle Questions
Say to children: *Choose one part of the story. Tell us what is happening in the part you chose and the feeling of the character.*

Afterwards, invite children to reflect by saying: *Think about what our circle shared. We heard about so many different parts and feelings. What did someone share that made you think, "I thought that, too"?*

Carryover Coaching
Use these additional prompts for one-on-one conferences.
- Notice when the character gets into trouble.
- Use the picture and words to think about what happened.
- Look at the picture. Ask: *What does the character's face show? What does her body show? How must she feel?*

SKILLS AND STANDARDS

Comprehension Skill:
Understand character

CCSS: RL.K.1, RL.K.3 • SL.K.1.A–B, SL.K.2, SL.K.6 • RL.1.1, RL.1.3 • SL.1.A, SL.1.2, SL.1.6

Social Justice:
JU.K-2.12 (I know when people are treated unfairly.)

CASEL:
Social Awareness
- Show concern for the feelings of others
- Demonstrate empathy and compassion

 # Heartwork

Strategy: Readers can pretend to be different characters and think about how each character might feel different on the same page.

As You Read . . .
- Pretend to be one character: Imagine you are doing what he/she does, seeing what he/she sees, and hearing what he/she hears. Think about how you feel as you pretend.
- Then, pretend to be another character. Imagine and feel again.
- Think about how the characters' feelings are the same or different and why.

Places to Pause
Pause on the page that shows the puppy jumping onto the boy's lap. Tell children that you want to see what is happening from inside the different characters. Pretend to be the dog. Model how you're using the picture to imagine you are in the scene. Share how jumping into the boy's lap makes you feel excited at first because you're so happy to be with him. Then, how you feel confused because he pushed you away. Then, switch places and pretend to be the boy. Think aloud about how having the dirty, smelly puppy on your lap feels gross and makes you angry. Share your thoughts on how the same scene can produce different feelings for different characters.

Circle Questions
Turn to the pages that show the dog shaking off the water and then knocking down the table. Say to children: *Let's look closely at these two pages. Choose a character—the boy, the dad, or the dog. What clues do you see in the pictures and the words that help you know what the character you chose is feeling?*

Afterwards, invite children to reflect by saying: *Think about what your friends were looking at to help them understand the characters' feelings. What might that make you want to do?*

Carryover Coaching
Use these additional prompts for one-on-one conferences.
- Choose a character and pretend to be that character.
- Use the picture to help you act out what is happening.
- Make the characters talk to you.
- Think about what you feel right now.
- Try another character.

Beyond the Book

Invite children to expand their emotional vocabulary. Having the language to articulate our own emotions and name the emotions of others is key to our ability to self-regulate and empathize. In her book, *Atlas of Heart,* Brené Brown writes, "Language is our portal to meaning-making, connection, healing, learning, and self-awareness. Having access to the right words can open up entire universes" (2022). The work of this section requires multiple sessions. Because most people (children and adults) narrow down their description of emotion to three words—*happy, sad,* and *mad*—we might start with the associated emotions tied to those words. Here's one way to introduce the meaning of a feeling word and help children associate the word with facial expressions and stories.

Say the feeling word to children and invite them to repeat the word with you, for example: *confident.* Then, share a child-friendly definition of the word. *(Feeling confident means feeling sure that you can do something well or you're sure you are right.)* Next, tell a story about a time when you felt the emotion. *(Let me think about a time I felt confident . . .)* Invite children to remember a story of the feeling, too. *(Think of a time when you felt sure about being able to do something.)* Share what the feeling might look like on our bodies. *(Let's picture what confident looks like on our bodies. What does your face look like? What does your body look like?)* Listen to and reinforce ideas, such as smiling, standing tall, and shoulders up. Have children practice sharing their own definitions of the word. *(Think about our stories around the word* confident. *If someone asked you what the word* confident *means, what would you say?)*

As an extension, create a growing chart through interactive writing with feeling words, child-created definitions, and drawings of people feeling that way. Invite children to illustrate their feeling-word stories.

A Few More Favorites

Mommy Sayang
by Rosana Sullivan

Just Ask!
by Sonia Sotomayor

A child's drawing after exploring the feeling word *guilty,* inspired by the moments after the boy yells at his dog and sees him curled up under the table.

First graders' definitions of *guilty:*

"When you hurt someone and your heart needs a band-aid."

— Samantha

"A heavy mucky feeling because you feel bad for doing something wrong."

— Tom

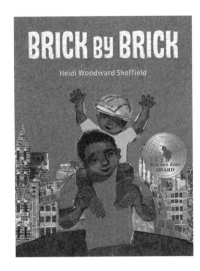

BRICK BY BRICK

Written and illustrated by Heidi Woodward Sheffield
Grades K–2 / Fiction

A Bit About the Book

Brick by Brick is a celebration of dreams, hard work, pride, and joy. In this heartwarming story, readers get to see a son's love and admiration of his father. Each day, Papi works hard as a bricklayer, building the city one brick at a time, while his son builds dreams of his own, reading book after book at school. Across the story, we see snippets of daily life for the boy and his father. As the book comes to an end, we celebrate a dream achieved as the family moves into a house that Papi built with his strong, loving hands. Every part of this reading experience is joyful—from the beauty of the textured collage illustrations to the playful language. Be sure to point out the use of both Spanish and English within the text and illustrations.

SKILLS AND STANDARDS

Comprehension Skill:
Make connections

CCSS: RL.K.1, RL.K.3, RL.K.7 • SL.K.1.A–B, SL.K.2, SL.K.6 • RL.1.1, RL.1.3, RL.1.7 • SL.1.1A, SL.1.2, SL.1.6 • RL.2.1 RL.2.3, RL.2.7 • SL.2.1.A, SL.2.2, SL.2.6

Social Justice:
DI.K-2.17 (I can describe some ways that I am similar to and different from people who share my identities and those who have other identities.)

CASEL:
Social Awareness
• Recognize strengths in others

 Identity

Strategy: Readers look for ways they are the same as the characters in books and say, "Me, too!"

As You Read . . .

- Look closely at the characters.
- Notice whether we look like a character on the outside (e.g., age, gender).
- Notice whether we are like a character on the inside—what we do, like, or want; how we speak; or what we care about.
- Ask: *How do the things I share with the characters help me understand them?*

Places to Pause

Pause on the page that shows Papi making the little boy breakfast. Use the picture to notice what Papi looks like and think aloud about whether you share any physical traits. Then, use the text and picture together to notice any similar interests, desires, languages, and so on. Talk about how connecting to a character also helps us understand that person.

Circle Questions

Return to the book and do a quick picture walk of its pages. Invite children to look for things they share with the character—on the inside and on the outside. Say: *Let's look back at the story. What do you share with the characters on the outside and on the inside?* Consider having children draw a picture of themselves and the character to show their connections. Have them complete this sentence stem: "I'm just like [character's name] because I . . ."

Afterwards, invite children to reflect by saying: *Think about what your friends and classmates shared. What new connections do you also see in your friends and classmates? Think about how you're also like some of your friends.*

Carryover Coaching

Use these additional prompts for one-on-one conferences.

- Look at the picture.
- Notice a character's outside parts. Look at size, age, skin color, and so on.
- Pay attention to what the character is doing.
- Pay attention to what the character likes.
- Pay attention to what the character wants and cares about.
- Ask yourself: *How am I the same as ___?*

A kindergartner's picture of himself and the little boy from the story. He shared, "We both have brown skin and like to make projects."

 # Harm and Healing

Strategy: Readers know that sometimes, instead of having problems, characters have dreams they are trying to achieve.

As You Read . . .

- Pay attention to something the character wants.
- Look for the things he does to help him get what he wants.
- Notice when he succeeds and how it makes him feel.

Places to Pause

Stop on the page that shows the little boy seeing his new house for the first time. Acknowledge that his dream has come true. Take a moment to revisit the page that shows him holding the picture of his "dream house" and remind children that he shared this wish earlier in the book. Then, go back to the page with the new house. Think aloud about all the things we saw his Papi do to make that dream a reality for his family. Talk about the surprise and joy the family felt in this moment of achieving that dream.

Circle Questions

Say to children: *Let's think about what makes this dream important to the little boy and his family. What makes them so happy about this new house?*

Afterwards, invite children to reflect by asking: *What ideas that your classmates shared stand out to you the most?*

Carryover Coaching

Use these additional prompts for one-on-one conferences.

- Look for words that tell what the character wants—*want, dream, hope, wish.*
- Pay attention to what the character does. Think: *How does that help him get what he wants?*
- Look at the picture. Ask: *What does his face show? What does his body show? How must he feel?*

SKILLS AND STANDARDS

Comprehension Skill:
Identify tone and mood

CCSS: RL.K.3, RL.K.4 • SL.K.1.A–B, SL.K.2, SL.K.6 • RL.1.3, RL.1.4 • SL.1.1.A, SL.1.2, SL.1.6 • RL.2.3, RL.2.4 • SL.2.1.A, SL.2.2, SL.2.6

Social Justice:
DI.K-2.9 (I know everyone has feelings, and I want to get along with people who are similar to and different from me.)

CASEL:
Social Awareness
- Show concern for the feelings of others

♥ Heartwork

Strategy: Readers can understand the story and the characters by paying attention to the words the author uses.

As You Read . . .

- Look for describing words or sentences.
- Close your eyes and use those words to picture and feel that part of the story.
- Think of a feeling word that fits the pictures in your mind.

Places to Pause

For this lesson, you might decide to highlight the sensory language with a colorful highlighter. A great page to highlight this feature is the one in which Papi mixes cement while the boy creates with clay. Show children the words *whirrrr, whoosh, splat,* and *pat.* Talk to them about the movie you make in your mind and what you feel with those words.

Another option is to highlight figurative language. Turn to the page that shows Papi picking up the boy from school. Draw students' attention to the simile, "Papi feels like the sun, hot and glistening." Discuss with children how this comparison helps you understand the boy's feelings for his dad.

Circle Questions

One of the most impactful ways to support vocabulary instruction is to make word consciousness and appreciation part of the classroom experience. This circle is all about fostering word consciousness. Revisit the book, inviting children to listen for favorite words within the text or hidden in the pictures. Ask children: *What word stood out most to you? Why?*

Afterwards, take the words that children named and turn them into a list poem. Then read the poem together to celebrate the book's language.

Carryover Coaching

Use these additional prompts for one-on-one conferences.
- Reread a part, looking at the words.
- Notice words that help you make a clear mind picture.
- Think about the feeling of that word. Ask: *How does it connect to the character's feelings? How does it make me feel?*

Beyond the Book

The languages we use are expressions of our cultures. One way we can celebrate cultures is to explore words and expressions in different languages. Say to children: *Today, we are going to celebrate other cultures by learning a little bit about how people talk to one another. Let's pick some places and look up how they say some of our favorite words.*

Begin by choosing some places around the world and looking up the languages spoken in those places. Then, ask children to turn to a partner and name some words or phrases they would like to learn to say in different languages. Children will often express interest in greetings and phrases, such as "Would you like to play?" Use Google Translate to learn how to say those phrases in different languages and have children practice saying those words aloud to one another. To extend this activity, have children choose one of their favorite words or phrases to share with friends or loved ones at home.

SKILLS AND STANDARDS

CASEL
Relationship Skills
- Demonstrate cultural competency

A Few More Favorites

The Oldest Student
by Rita Lorraine Hubbard

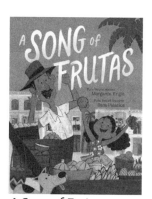

A Song of Frutas
by Margarita Engle

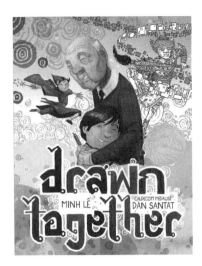

DRAWN TOGETHER

Written by Minh Lê / Illustrated by Dan Santat

Grades 1–2 / Fiction / #OwnVoices

A Bit About the Book

While spending the day at his grandfather's house, the main character struggles to find ways to connect due to language barriers. He speaks English, and his grandfather speaks Thai. When words offer no solution, the boy and his grandfather try to find an activity they can share together. Through trial and error, they finally discover something they both deeply enjoy and can engage in to create new memories. They find that their art can bridge the gap between them that words could not. This is a story about connection, cultures, and multigenerational relationships that build and grow through a foundation of shared experiences.

SKILLS AND STANDARDS

Comprehension Skill:
Infer about characters and relationships

CCSS: RL.1.1, RL.1.3 • SL.1.1, SL.1.2 • RL.2.1, RL.2.3 • SL.2.1, SL.2.2

Social Justice:
DI.K-2.7 (I can describe some ways that I am similar to and different from people who share my identities and those who have other identities.)

CASEL:
Social Awareness
• Integrate personal and social identities
• Link feelings, values, and thoughts
• Recognize strengths in others

Identity

Strategy: Readers know that our identities are a combination of many things, including our interests, experiences, culture, language, and families. Our identities help us connect with others through shared similarities and interests.

As You Read . . .

- Observe the similarities and differences between the characters.
- Ask: *What are some pieces of the characters' identities?*
- Reflect on the characters' identities and share about what they have in common in terms of their identities.

Places to Pause

Pause on the page in which the grandfather brings out his sketchbook. Review the previous few pages to notice the characters' expressions as they engage in various activities. Share what you notice about their interests in food, television, activities. Compare that to their reactions when the grandfather sets his sketchbook on the table. Ask: *What does this say about the characters' identities?*

Circle Questions

The main character and his grandfather connect through a shared interest that they hold as part of their identity. Say to children: *Think about a time when you connected with someone special in this way. With whom did you connect? What part of your identity did you find you shared?*

Afterwards, invite children to reflect by asking: *What did someone share that made you think, "Me, too"?*

Carryover Coaching

Use these additional prompts for one-on-one conferences.

- Look closely at the pages.
- Look at the characters' faces as they change across the pages.
- Think about what a character might be feeling at those moments of change.
- List words to describe the main character's feelings.

 Harm and Healing

Strategy: Readers can learn lessons by watching how characters build connections.

As You Read . . .

- Notice what problems the characters were facing. How did the characters fix the problem?
- Look at the things each character did and the ways each one acted.
- Ask: *What can that teach me about how to act and what to do in real life?*

Places to Pause

Pause on the two pages that show the characters in "illustration form" where the boy says, "We see each other for the first time." Review the following pages up to where he says, " . . . and we build a new world that even words can't describe." Share your thoughts about the main character's change of feelings about his relationship with his grandfather. Point out the moments in his illustrations that show their relationship changing.

Circle Questions

Say to children: *Let's think about the relationship between the main character and his grandfather from the beginning of the book to the end. What do you think the boy learned throughout this story?*

Afterwards, invite children to reflect by asking: *What did someone share that you also thought about already? What did someone share that you hadn't thought of yet?*

Carryover Coaching

Use these additional prompts for one-on-one conferences.

- Find a place where the characters' relationship grows.
- Ask: *What's happening?*
- Look for what changed.
- Name how the expression on each character's face changes over time.

 **Heartwork**

Strategy: Readers notice how authors and illustrators can show feelings in the ways they design the illustrations.

As You Read . . .
• Notice the ways the illustrator's art style changes—comic book–style images and illustrative art—over the pages.
• Think about what is happening in the story.
• Ask: *How do these changes represent the characters' feelings and experiences?*

Places to Pause
Pause on the two pages in which the characters run toward each other across the bridge. Turn to the last page, where the boy shares that he and his grandfather are "happily speechless." Think aloud about the message and meaning the author shares with us through these words.

Circle Questions
Say to children: *On the last page, we see the main character and his grandfather smile at each other while holding their drawing tools. We know that this relationship between the two characters has changed to a positive connection for both. Think about what feelings might have changed inside of the characters' hearts when their relationship grew and became stronger. Think of your own relationships. What was a moment when you felt a change in your heart to a stronger feeling of connection?* You might offer this sentence stem: "I felt a bigger connection when I . . ."

Afterwards, invite children to reflect by asking: *What did you hear that taught you something new?*

Carryover Coaching
Use these additional prompts for one-on-one conferences.
• Think about a character's feelings at the end of the story.
• Think back to a time when they felt like this.
• Feel that feeling again.
• Pretend they're the character.
• Feel the character's feelings as they think about his experience.

Beyond the Book

Offer children a chance to express gratitude for their connection to someone close to them. Invite them to create a letter to share with that special person. They can also create illustrations and add colors, as inspired by the book. Their letters may be about a shared identity or a shared experience. If possible, have children share their letters with their loved ones. You can mail the letters, too!

SKILLS AND STANDARDS

CASEL
Social Awareness
• Recognize strengths in others
• Understand and express gratitude

A child shares about a connection with a special someone

A Few More Favorites

What We'll Build
by Oliver Jeffers

Hair Love
by Matthew A. Cherry

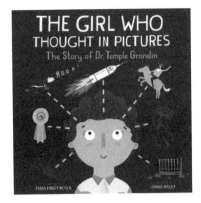

THE GIRL WHO THOUGHT IN PICTURES:

The Story of Dr. Temple Grandin

Written by Julia Finley Mosca / Illustrated by Daniel Rieley
Grades 1–2 / Nonfiction

A Bit About the Book

This picture book biography tells the inspirational story of scientist Temple Grandin and how she contributed to compassionate farming practices. Using a child-friendly rhyming pattern, the book begins in Temple's early years when she was diagnosed with autism and doctors told her parents that she wouldn't talk or do much of anything. The book goes on to show how, with a little belief in herself, some wonderful mentors, and her unique ways of seeing the world, Grandin changed farming forever. For readers who may want to study her life further, this book offers more learning opportunities with a timeline, an interview, and additional resource pages at the end.

SKILLS AND STANDARDS

Comprehension Skill:
Infer about a character's identity through his/her strengths and weaknesses

CCSS: RL.1.3, RI.1.3 • SL.1.1.A, SL.1.2, SL.1.6 • RL.2.3, RI.2.3 • SL.2.1.A, SL.2.2, SL.2.6

Social Justice:
ID.K-2.3 (I know that all my group identities are part of me—but that I am always ALL me.)

CASEL:
Self-Awareness
• Identify one's emotions
• Develop interests and a sense of purpose

Identity

Strategy: Readers learn about a person's identity by paying attention to things that are hard for her as well as things she is good at.

As You Read . . .

• Look for parts in the story in which the character feels frustrated or has a hard time with something.
• Find other parts that show the character doing something well or easily.
• Think about how both strengths and challenges are part of that character's life and identity.

Places to Pause

Pause on the page that shows Temple having a tantrum. Talk about the things that made her feel frustrated—loud noises, itchy clothes, and talking. Share with children how seeing this helps you understand more about her. Then, turn to the page that shows Temple with a rocket. Point out things she's good at—science, inventions, and so on. Share how you understand more about her by looking at her strengths, too.

Circle Questions

Say to children: *Readers, we know that big feelings sometimes show up when we are doing hard things or when we are doing things that we are good at. Let's think about things that we are good at and things that are hard for us. Pick a "good at" or hard thing for you and tell us what it is and how it makes you feel.* Invite children to use the sentence stem: "I'm good at ___. It makes me feel . . ." or "___ is hard for me. When I am ___, sometimes I feel . . ."

Afterwards, invite children to reflect by asking: *What did someone share that made you think, "Me, too"?*

Carryover Coaching

Use these additional prompts for one-on-one conferences.

- Look closely at the character's face.
- Find a part in which she feels frustrated.
- Think: *What makes this hard? How does she feel?*
- Find a part in which she is doing great.
- Think: *What makes it easy? How does she feel?*

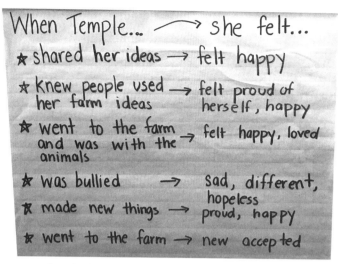

When Temple... ⟶ she felt...
- ★ shared her ideas → felt happy
- ★ knew people used her farm ideas → felt proud of herself, happy
- ★ went to the farm and was with the animals → felt happy, loved
- ★ was bullied → sad, different, hopeless
- ★ made new things → proud, happy
- ★ went to the farm → new accepted

Second grade ideas from a sharing circle

 Harm and Healing

Strategy: Readers think about the subject of a biography and how she made things better for others.

As You Read . . .

- Think about what the subject did, changed, or tried to change.
- Ask: *Who did this help? How did it help her?*
- Celebrate the subject: *Hooray!*

Places to Pause

Pause on the page that shows the cow web. Share how Temple understood that farmers were not treating cows kindly. Talk about how the red lines led to ways the cows were hurt and the green lines led to how Temple helped them. Celebrate Temple and how she made life for farm animals better by designing new ways for cows to move and stay calm.

Circle Questions

Say to children: *In this story, we read about how Temple helped farm animals. Think of something good that Temple did. Let's circle up to celebrate her and what she did. We'll end our circle with a "Hooray, Temple!" cheer.* Some possible sentence stems you might share with children include: "Temple helped . . ." or "Temple was/is . . ." or "Temple made . . ."

Afterwards, invite children to reflect by saying: *Think about what your classmates shared about all the ways Temple made a difference. What stays with you most? How might she inspire you, too?*

SKILLS AND STANDARDS

Comprehension Skill: Identify problems and motivations

CCSS: RL.1.1, RL.1.2, RL.1.6, RI.1.1, RI.1.6 • SL.1.1.A, SL.1.2, SL.1.6 • RL.2.1, RL.2.2, RL.2.6, RI.2.1, RI.2.6 • SL.2.1.A, SL.2.2, SL.2.6

Social Justice:
AC.K-2.16 (I care about those who are treated unfairly.)
AC.K-2.17 (I can and will do something when I see unfairness—this includes telling an adult.)

CASEL:
Relationship Skills
- Show leadership in groups
- Seek or offer support and help when needed
- Stand up for the rights of others

Responsible Decision-Making
- Reflect on one's role to promote personal, family, and community well-being

Carryover Coaching

Use these additional prompts for one-on-one conferences.

- Think: *What made this person famous?*
- Find a part in which the person makes a change.
- Use pictures and words. Think: *Why did she want to help/change something?*
- Use the pictures and words to look for who is being helped. Ask: *What is easier for them?*

SKILLS AND STANDARDS

Comprehension Skill:
Infer about character

CCSS: RL.1.1, RL.1.3 RL.1.6, RI.1.1, RI.1.6 • SL1.1.A, SL.1.2, SL.1.6 • RL.2.1, RL.2.3, RL.2.6, RI.2.1, RI.2.6 • SL.2.1A, SL.2.2, SL.2.6

Social Justice:
DI.K-2.8 (I want to know about other people and how our lives and experiences are the same and different.)

CASEL:
Social Awareness
- Take others' perspectives
- Demonstrate empathy and compassion
- Show concern for the feelings of others

Heartwork

Strategy: Readers can gain insight into the feelings of characters by pretending to be them.

As You Read . . .

- Picture yourself in the character's place.
- Pretend what happened to her is happening to you.
- Feel her feelings with your heart.

Places to Pause

Pause on the page that shows someone throwing papers at Temple. Model for children how to close your eyes and picture yourself in Temple's place. Pretend that you're being teased and act out being hit by papers. Think aloud about what you feel and imagine what she must also feel.

Circle Questions

Tell children you are going to reread the book aloud. This time, they will pretend they are Temple. Read the book and pause every couple of pages to give children time to pretend. Then, circle up and ask children to share one part of the story and the feeling that was in their hearts when they pretended to be Temple. Offer the sentence stem: "When I pretended . . . , I felt . . ." (For example: "When I pretended I was getting teased at school, I felt sad and hurt. I think Temple was sad and hurt, too.")

Afterwards, invite children to reflect by asking: *What ideas that were shared stand out to you most? How does this help you understand Temple's life and experiences?*

Carryover Coaching

Use these additional prompts for one-on-one conferences.

- Look at a character's picture and imagine you are that character.
- Act out what is happening, pretending to be the character.
- Think: *What am I feeling in my heart as I pretend?*

 **Beyond the Book**

Supporting children with self-regulation techniques is an important part of social and emotional learning. Facing moments that are hard or frustrating for us is an unavoidable part of life, but feeling that something is hard doesn't have to ruin our day. It doesn't even have to mean we stop trying. We need a self-regulation technique to center us. In this technique, we teach children to tense their muscles and then release the tension. Using this strategy can help children lower their heart rates and even their cortisol levels and find their way back to calm.

Say to children: *In this book, we saw there were times when Temple felt upset or frustrated. We know that we can feel frustrated and upset sometimes, too. Let's practice something that we can do when we feel this way. This is called "Squeeze and Relax." First, let's squeeze our hands super tight, breathe in, and hold it for a few seconds.* (Count to five.) *Now, let's breathe out and relax our hands again. We can do this with different body parts until we feel calm again.*

After this exercise, invite children to share how they feel.

A Few More Favorites

Magic Ramen
by Andrea Wang

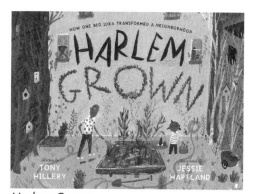

Harlem Grown
by Tony Hillery

SKILLS AND STANDARDS

CASEL
Self-Management
• Manage one's emotions
• Identify and use stress-
  management strategies

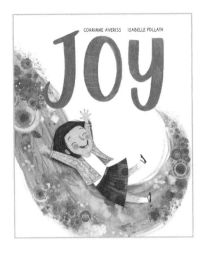

JOY

Written by Corrinne Averiss / Illustrated by Isabelle Follath
Grades 1–2 / Fiction

A Bit About the Book

Fern is a sweet little girl who loves everything about her Nanna—from the silly mice decoration on her mantlepiece to the bright smile that often lights up her face. But one day, Fern notices that the light in her Nanna seems to have gone out. Fern's mother says that Nanna has lost her joy. This news sends Fern on an adventure to "catch" joy for her Nanna once again. With gorgeous illustrations, this story of compassion and empathy will help young readers understand how characters and people can spread kindness and love.

SKILLS AND STANDARDS

Comprehension Skill:
Infer about character

CCSS: RL.1.1, RL.1.3 • SL.1.1.A, SL.1.2, SL.1.6, • RL.2.1, RL.2.3 • SL.2.1.A, SL.2.2, SL.2.6

Social Justice:
JU.K-2.11 (I know my friends have many identities, but they are always still just themselves.)

CASEL:
Social Awareness
• Recognize strengths in others

Identity

Strategy: Readers think about family as part of a character's identity.

As You Read . . .

- Choose a character.
- Name the role of the character in the family—parent, child, grandparent.
- Think: *What does the character do in that role? What kind of person is this character?* (e.g., helpful grandchild, kind mom)

Places to Pause

Pause on the page that starts with Fern thinking that Nanna deserves some "whooosh." Name Fern's family identities during your think aloud—daughter, granddaughter, and so on. Then, remind children about some of the things Fern does as a granddaughter—visits Nanna, spends time with her, wants to make her happy, and goes to catch joy for her. Lastly, think aloud about what Fern does in her granddaughter role and what it teaches us about her.

Circle Questions

Pair this circle with Shared Writing. Invite children to think about Fern as a granddaughter. In the first round, have them come up with a word to describe Fern as a granddaughter. (*Fern is a ___ granddaughter.*) On your Shared Writing chart, choose one of the words to complete the first sentence. Then, in the second round, have children think about one thing that Fern did in the story to show that she is that kind of granddaughter. (*She ___.*) For example: *Fern is a sweet granddaughter. She tried to catch chuckles for her Nanna.*

Afterwards, invite children to reflect by saying: *Think of all the different ways your classmates saw the main character. What did someone share that helped you see this character in a brand-new way? What did someone share that matched your thought?*

Carryover Coaching

Use these additional prompts for one-on-one conferences.

- Find the character's family members.
- Look for what the character does with this family member.
- Think about what the family member and character are doing now.
- Look at how the character makes this family member feel.
- Find a word to describe the kind of (family member) this character is.

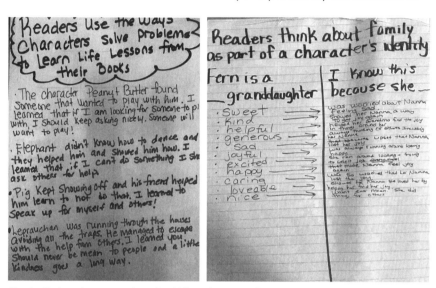

Charts that capture second graders' ideas during circle experiences.

 Harm and Healing

Strategy: Readers use the ways characters solve problems to learn life lessons from their books.

As You Read . . .

- Find a way the character fixed a problem.
- Look at the things the character did and the ways she acted.
- Ask: *What can that teach me about how to act and what to do in real life?*

Places to Pause

Focus on the last few pages that show Fern and Nanna at the park together. Share your thoughts about how Nanna's joy returned when Fern showed her how much she meant to her and spent time with her. Point out the things they do together in the park—enjoy the birds and butterflies and go on a picnic. Then, share how you might bring joy to others by doing some of the same things Fern did—by showing you care, spending time with someone, and so on.

Circle Questions

Say to children: *Bring a favorite book with you to the circle. Tell how a character fixed a problem and what you want to do to be more like that*

SKILLS AND STANDARDS

Comprehension Skill:
Determine themes

CCSS: RL.1.1, RL.1.2 • SL.1.1.A, SL.1.2, SL.1.6 • RL.2.1, RL.2.2 • SL.2.1.A, SL.2.2, SL.2.6

Social Justice:
AC.K-2.18 (I will say something or tell an adult if someone is being hurtful, and will do my part to be kind even if I don't like something they say or do.)

CASEL:
Responsible Decision-Making
- Anticipate and evaluate the consequences of one's actions
- Identify solutions for personal and social problems

character. You night offer these sentence stems: "My character . . . I learned that I can/should also . . ."

Afterwards, invite children to reflect by asking: *What idea did you hear that sounded like good advice? What lesson are you left thinking about?*

Carryover Coaching
Use these additional prompts for one-on-one conferences.

- Find the fix part. Pay attention to what the character did to fix the problem.
- Think about how the character's choice helped.
- Say: *When someone is* [name the problem], *you can help by* [name something you learned from what the character did].

SKILLS AND STANDARDS

Comprehension Skill:
Identify tone and mood

CCSS: RL.1.1, RL.1.7 • SL.1.1.A, SL.1.2, SL.1.6 • RL.2.1, RL.2.7 • SL.2.1.A, SL.2.2, SL.2.6

Social Justice:
DI.K-2.9 (I know everyone has feelings, and I want to get along with people who are similar to and different from me.)

CASEL:
Social Awareness:
- Demonstrate empathy and compassion
- Show concern for the feelings of others

❤ Heartwork

Strategy: Readers notice how authors and illustrators show feelings in a book in the ways they create pictures.

As You Read . . .
- Look for changes in the colors and brightness of the page.
- Think about what is happening in the story.
- Ask: *How do the color and the picture match the feeling of the page?*

Places to Pause
Pause on the page that tells readers that Nanna has stopped doing the things she enjoys. Point out how the picture looks very different from the one before. In the earlier picture of Nanna's house, we see bright colors. In this picture, everything has become dull and gray. The plants have drooped, the pictures are crooked, and the mice have webs on them. In this part, Nanna feels dull and gray, too. She is sad. The picture's colors seem to reflect Nanna's feelings and the feeling of the page.

Circle Questions
Say to children: *Think about how the illustrator showed feelings in the pictures. Choose a feeling that might go in one of your own stories. What colors might you use to show that feeling? What might you add to the picture to show that feeling, too?*

Afterwards, invite children to reflect by asking: *What new thing can you try when you're writing or illustrating stories?*

Carryover Coaching
Use these additional prompts for one-on-one conferences.

- Study a picture.
- Look closely at the colors and details.

- Notice the feeling the picture gives them.
- Look at the characters' feelings on the page.

📖 Beyond the Book

One way to celebrate each person's uniqueness is by understanding that we enjoy different things. This activity invites children to notice the joys in each other's lives and to tap into what brings them joy as well.

Say to children: *In the story, Fern tries to capture joy and bring it back to her grandmother. But Fern soon learns that we can't bottle up joy. Joy is found in the happiness that certain things in life bring to our hearts, and everyone has different things that bring them joy. Joy can be found in spending time with people and doing different activities. Let's think of things that bring us joy and capture our joy in a picture!*

SKILLS AND STANDARDS

CASEL
Social Awareness
- Understand and express gratitude

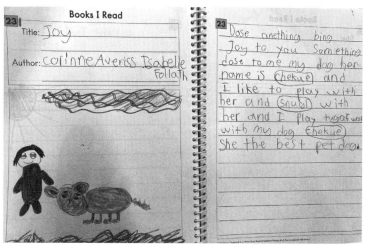

Second graders sketch and jot ideas to get ready for a circle share.

A Few More Favorites

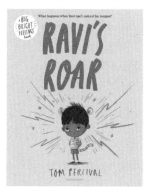

Ravi's Roar
by Tom Percival

Between Us and Abuela
by Mitali Perkins

LAXMI'S MOOCH

Written by Shelly Anand / Illustrated by Nabi H. Ali
Grades K–1 / Fiction / #OwnVoices

A Bit About the Book

In this moving story of self-love, Laxmi, a young Indian American girl, becomes aware of her *mooch*, the Hindi word for mustache. It all begins during recess one day when her friends tell her she'd be the perfect cat, due to her whiskers. Laxmi, taken aback as she begins to find hair all over her body, is at first devastated and ashamed. However, with a little help from her mother, Laxmi comes to embrace her body hair, and then helps her friends see the beauty of a mooch! **Note:** Don't miss the picture glossary of Hindi vocabulary at the back of the book.

 **Identity**

Strategy: Readers know that our identities are a mix of what we look like on the outside and who we are on the inside. We think of both as we learn about characters.

As You Read . . .

• Think about the words used to describe the character. Look at the pictures to see what the character looks like.
• Think about what the character does and what she is like as a person (e.g., basic traits).
• List words that tell us about the person's outside and inside.

Places to Pause

Pause on the page that shows Laxmi offering to draw a mooch on Noah. Think aloud as you zoom in on Laxmi and list some of her physical traits. Talk to children about how these traits help us picture her in our minds. Then, think aloud about her action of offering to make a mooch for Noah. Consider what that says about her on the inside. List an outside (physical) and inside trait as you name parts of Laxmi's identity.

Circle Questions

Say to children: *After reading this book, we got to know a little bit about Laxmi. Let's think of some words that describe her. We can add words that describe what she is like on the outside and the inside.* Collect these words to co-create an identity web for Laxmi.

Afterwards, invite children to reflect by asking: *What did you hear that helped you see something new about Laxmi?*

Carryover Coaching

Use these additional prompts for one-on-one conferences.

- Look closely at the page.
- Look at a character. Notice what the character looks like.
- Think about what the person says and does.
- List words to describe this person.

Harm and Healing

Strategy: Readers look for problems by finding moments when characters' feelings change to upset feelings.

As You Read . . .

- Notice when the character's feelings change to sad, mad, embarrassed, or frustrated.
- Think about what happened right before that change.
- Ask: *What caused this feeling? Is there a new problem for the character?*

Places to Pause

Pause on the two pages that show Laxmi in the bathroom and then sitting at her desk. Think aloud about how we see her beginning to get upset. Notice her pink cheeks, her downward-set eyebrows, and the fact that she has begun to hide her mouth. Then consider what caused the change—the children pointing out her "whiskers" caused her to be embarrassed and ashamed.

Circle Questions

Say to children: *We can notice people's feelings in lots of different ways. Let's think about what showed us that Laxmi had a problem. What helped you see her hurt feelings?*

Afterwards, invite children to reflect by asking: *What ideas that were shared stand out to you most?*

Carryover Coaching

Use these additional prompts for one-on-one conferences.

- Find when a character's feelings change to hurt or upset.
- Look at the pictures to see the character's feelings.
- Reread the part before this.
- Think about what caused the upset feelings and name the cause as a problem.

SKILLS AND STANDARDS

Comprehension Skills:
Identify cause and effect; identify problems

CCSS: RL.K.1, RL,K.3 • SL.K.1.1.A–B, SL.K.2, SL.K.6 • RL.1.1, RL.1.3 • SL.1.1.A, SL.1.2, SL.1.6

Social Justice:
DI.K-2.9 (I know everyone has feelings, and I want to get along with people who are similar to and different from me.)

CASEL:
Social Awareness
- Demonstrate empathy and compassion
- Show concern for the feelings of others

 Heartwork

Strategy: Readers feel empathy for characters by remembering times when they have had similar feelings.

As You Read . . .
- Name the feeling of the character.
- Remember a time when you have felt that way. Hold that feeling in your heart.
- Feel the feeling with the character as you think about what happened to her.

Places to Pause
Pause on the page that shows Laxmi on the playground. Tell children that we see Laxmi feeling embarrassed. Have them think back to a moment from their own lives when they have also felt embarrassed. Think aloud about how remembering your own moment can help you connect to Laxmi's feelings, even though your experiences may be different. Share how as you read, you can have a similar feeling and better understand how Laxmi feels.

Circle Questions
Say to children: *Zoom in on a part of the story that holds a big feeling for Laxmi. Think of a moment when you've shared that feeling. Hold that feeling in your heart for a moment and tell us about it.*

Afterwards, invite children to reflect by asking: *What story did someone share that made you think, "Something like that happened to me, too"?*

Carryover Coaching
Use these additional prompts for one-on-one conferences.
- Think about the character's feelings right now.
- Think back to a time when you have felt the same way.
- Feel that feeling again.
- Pretend you're the character.
- Feel her feelings as you think about what is happening to her.

Beyond the Book

Say to children: *In this story, we can see Laxmi's physical reaction to the hurt she felt while playing with her friends. In moments of hurt, embarrassment, or fear, we can feel out of control. However, we can take back that control by learning ways to bring our bodies back to feeling calm. There are things we can do to make our bodies feel better again. This is called* regulation. *One way to do that is by slow breathing. Let's try it.*

Prompt children to take one slow deep breath in while lifting their arms in the air. Count slowly to three as they breathe in. Then count to four as they hold their breath. Finally, count to four again as you have children lower their arms and breathe out slowly. Repeat this process three times. Invite children to share how their bodies feel at the end of the exercise.

Children practicing their deep breathing

A Few More Favorites

Sulwe
by Lupita Nyong'o

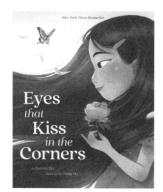

Eyes That Kiss in the Corners
by Joanna Ho

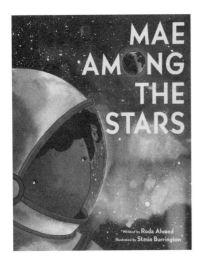

MAE AMONG THE STARS

Written by Roda Ahmed / Illustrated by Stasia Burrington
Grades K–2 / Nonfiction / #OwnVoices

A Bit About the Book

This empowering story begins with Mae, a little girl who dreams of seeing Earth from space. With courage and support from her parents, she sets her sights on becoming an astronaut when she grows up. With so much joy and motivation, she begins to share this dream with her loved ones, all of whom are very supportive of Mae's hopes and desires. One day, when Mae shared with her class her aspirations to become an astronaut, her teacher tells her discouragingly that she is much better off pursuing something else. However, with resilience and determination as well as loving parents who support her dreams, Mae perseveres and continues to soar to become an astronaut.

 **Identity**

Strategy: Readers learn about a character's identity by looking at her goals, dreams, and interests.

As You Read . . .

• Look closely at the character's actions.
• Notice the words and expressions on the character's face when she takes action and engages in dialogue with other characters.
• Ask: *What do we know about the character's identity from our observations?*

Places to Pause

Pause on the pages in which Mae dreams she is floating in space. Mae is very enthusiastic about space, and she asks her parents to support her with her dreams. Review the things Mae does throughout the pages. Think aloud about the actions Mae takes as she remains determined to follow her dream of going to space. Ask: *What does this say about Mae and parts of her identity?*

Circle Questions

Say to children: *Throughout the story, we see that Mae dreams of becoming an astronaut and takes steps to make her dreams come true. Her parents support her, and they help her take the actions needed to pursue her goals. What are some of the things we learn about Mae and her identity?* You might offer children sentence stems, such as: "Mae is . . ." or "Mae loves to . . ."

Afterwards, invite children to reflect by saying: *Think about a time when you took actions to make a dream come true. What was your dream and what actions did you take?*

Carryover Coaching

Use these additional prompts for one-on-one conferences.

- Look closely at the pictures.
- Look closely at the words.
- Think: *What actions does the character take?*
- Share one thing you noticed about the character's actions.
- Ask: *How does this connect to their identity?*

Harm and Healing

Strategy: Readers know that sometimes harm is caused by the actions or words of others.

As You Read . . .

- Notice where in the story the character's feelings change to upset.
- Look at the expressions on the character's face.
- Ask: *What happened that caused the character to feel this way?*

Places to Pause

Pause at the parts of the book in which Mae feels upset (as she rides in the car on her way home from school and when her mother hugs her while Mae cries). Think aloud: *How does Mae feel right now? How is this different from how she felt at the beginning of the book?* Ask children: *What do you think caused Mae's feelings to change?*

Circle Questions

Say to children: *Through part of the story, we notice Mae's excitement and interest in following her dreams to become an astronaut. But then Mae's feelings change, and she begins to question if she can actually become an astronaut. Let's look at the page where Mae shares with her class about her dreams and read about her teacher's response. Think about how another character's words have impacted Mae and share your thoughts about it.*

Afterwards, invite children to reflect by asking: *What did you feel when this character's feelings changed? Think of a time you might have felt the same way as Mae.*

Carryover Coaching

Use these additional prompts for one-on-one conferences.

- Find a part in which the character's feelings change.
- Use the pictures to notice the character's expressions change.
- Find what happened right before to cause the character to change.

 **Heartwork**

Strategy: Readers can understand the story's problem and solution through the characters' actions.

As You Read . . .

- Look for how the characters interact with one another when presented with a problem.
- Notice how the characters' feelings change.
- Think: *What actions do the characters take to find a solution to the problem?*

Places to Pause

Pause on the page in which Mae's mother comforts her and wipes away her tears. Notice how her mother continues to encourage Mae with her words and gives her support and courage. Think aloud: *How does this make Mae feel? How did this change the way Mae felt after she talked to her teacher?* Ask children: *What actions does Mae take after receiving love and guidance from her mother?*

Circle Questions

Say to children: *Thinking about Mae's hopes and dreams, we see she is determined, and her parents support her. Let's think about what Mae experienced. Think about her change in feelings after her teacher told her to be a nurse instead. Then think about how her mother continued to support her and helped her stay determined. What can Mae's story teach the readers of this story?* Provide children with a sentence stem, such as: "Mae's story teaches us to . . ."

Afterwards, invite children to reflect by saying: *Share about a time when someone supported you with your hopes and dreams, or a time when you were upset and someone helped to cheer you up.*

Carryover Coaching

Use these additional prompts for one-on-one conferences.

- Find a moment when the characters find a solution to the problem.
- Use the pictures to notice a change in the characters' expressions.
- Put yourself in the character's place.
- Ask yourself: *What do I feel? How do I feel after interacting with a character who is helping?*

 **Beyond the Book**

This true story offers us a glimpse into the real-life experience of Dr. Mae Jemison, the first Black female astronaut. After reading this story, you may want to read other books about and watch videos of Dr. Jemison to give children more opportunities to connect with her and learn about all the things she has accomplished. She earned her MD, became an astronaut, and speaks three languages!

Mae had big dreams at a young age. Children feel their opportunities are endless, and we can support them in pursuing their dreams. Have children brainstorm about their hopes and dreams, then invite them to draw, design, or write about their big aspirations. Encourage them to share with the class and ask them how you, as their teacher, can support them.

Children draw about their hopes and dreams after being inspired by *Mae Among the Stars.*

A Few More Favorites

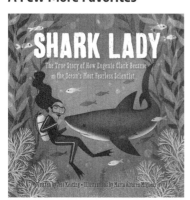

Shark Lady
by Jess Keating

The Girl With a Mind for Math
by Julia Finley Mosca

MILO IMAGINES THE WORLD

Written by Matt de la Peña / Illustrated by Christian Robinson
Grades 1–2 / Fiction

A Bit About the Book

As Milo takes his monthly subway ride to visit his mother in prison, he experiences lots of big feelings. To pass the time and calm his nerves, Milo shifts into a world of imagination. He begins to dream up whole worlds for passengers on the train and captures their imagined lives in his drawings. When one little boy, whom he pictured as living an extravagant life in a castle, steps off the train and heads toward the same place as him, Milo realizes that his first impressions may have led him to make assumptions.

SKILLS AND STANDARDS

Comprehension Skill:
Infer about character

CCSS: RL.1.1, RL.1.3 • SL.1.1.A, SL.1.2, SL.1.6 • RL.2.1, RL.2.3 • SL.2.1.A, SL.2.2, SL.2.6

Social Justice:
AC.K-2.16 (I care about those who are treated unfairly.)
AC.K-2.19 (I will speak up or do something if people are being unfair, even if my friends do not.)

CASEL:
Self-Awareness
• Show concern for the feelings of others
• Recognize strengths in others
Responsible Decision-Making
• Reflect on one's role to promote personal, family, and community well-being

 **Identity**

Strategy: Readers look for other people in a book that help the character fix problems or feel better.

As You Read . . .

- Pay attention to the people in the main character's life.
- Ask: *What do they do for/with the main character? How do they help?*
- Think about how those people help and make the main character feel.

Places to Pause

Pause on the page that shows Milo and his sister standing in line to see their mother. Think aloud about how Milo has an older sister to share this experience with. Talk about how she shares similar feelings and how, by holding his hand, she is there for him. Then, name how having this older sister can help Milo feel more comfortable when he's nervous.

Circle Questions

Say to children: *Choose two characters from the story. What is something one character did for/with the other character to make him or her feel better?* Offer this sentence stem: "When [character's name] ___, it helped ___ because ___." (For example: "When Milo gave his mom the picture, it helped his mom because she knew how much Milo loved her.")

Afterwards, invite children to reflect by asking: *What did someone share that helped you see something in a brand-new way?*

Carryover Coaching

Use these additional prompts for one-on-one conferences.

- Look at the characters around the main character.
- Use the pictures to notice how these other characters act with the main character.
- Use the words to notice what they do for the character.
- Think: *How does this help?*

 # Harm and Healing

Strategy: Readers notice what characters do when they are upset. Then they think about how this action helps or hurts.

As You Read . . .

- Look for a place where the character is upset or dealing with a problem.
- Think: *What does the character do next?*
- Ask: *How did this help or make it worse?*

Places to Pause

Pause on the page that shows Milo on the subway as he first begins to draw. Talk to children about Milo's "shook-up soda" feeling. Then, tell them how we can pay attention to what he chooses to draw next. Share how drawing may be one way Milo makes himself calmer and how this can help him feel better.

Circle Questions

Say to children: *Think about Milo's monthly subway rides to visit his mom.* (Reread this page to children and point out the many feelings Milo names.) *Why do you think Milo has the "shook-up soda" feeling?*

Afterwards, invite children to reflect by asking: *What do you now wonder about or want to learn more about?*

Carryover Coaching

Use these additional prompts for one-on-one conferences.

- Find a part in which the character feels upset.
- Read on. Find out what the character does next.
- Look at the picture. Think about what the character is doing here.
- Ask: *Did that make the character feel better or worse? Why?*

SKILLS AND STANDARDS

Comprehension Skill:
Identify problem and solution

CCSS: RL.1.1, RL.1.3 • SL.1.1.A, SL.1.2, SL.1.6 • RL.2.1, RL.2.3 • SL.2.1.A, SL.2.2, SL.2.6

Social Justice:
JU.K-2.14 (I know that life is easier for some people and harder for others and the reasons for that are not always fair.)

CASEL:
Self-Management
- Manage one's emotions
- Identify and use stress-management strategies
Relationship Skills
- Resolve conflicts constructively

 **Heartwork**

Strategy: Readers look for moments when characters learned a lesson and think about what that can teach them, too.

As You Read . . .
• Find a moment when the character fixed a mistake.
• Ask: *What did he do? What did he learn from that mistake?*
• Think: *What can that teach me, too?*

Places to Pause
Pause on the page that shows Milo reimagining all his pictures. Share your thinking about how the assumptions Milo made were wrong. Talk about how Milo fixed his mistake by reimagining other possibilities for those people and how he learned not to judge or make assumptions based on how someone looks. Then think aloud about how Milo's mistake can teach us about making assumptions, too.

Circle Questions
Say to children: *Think about Milo imagining his pictures differently. (Revisit those pages.) What is something Milo learned in the story or something you learned because of what happened in the book?* Offer one of these sentence stems: "I learned . . ." or "Milo learned . . ."

Afterwards, invite children to reflect by asking: *What ideas that were shared stand out to you most?*

Carryover Coaching
Use these additional prompts for one-on-one conferences.
• Look for an "uh-oh" part in which the character makes a mistake or does something wrong.
• Ask: *How does his mistake affect him? How does it affect others?*
• Notice how the character feels. Name the feeling.
• Ask: *What does he do differently?*
• Name a lesson learned.

Children jot down lessons they learned from *Milo Imagines the World.*

Beyond the Book

Milo learned a lesson about making assumptions about people based on their looks. Have children step into Milo's shoes and choose another character from the subway. Invite them to imagine one thing about the person or his/her life. Then have children turn to a partner and share their ideas. Afterwards, list some of their ideas to share with the class. Be sure to include very different ideas to emphasize that the possibilities are limitless. Remind children that our first impressions of people don't give us enough information to know what their lives are like. Repeat this process a few times. To extend this activity, invite children to draw a version of the person's story, just like Milo did.

SKILLS AND STANDARDS

CASEL
Relationship Skills
• Demonstrate cultural competency

A Few More Favorites

Mama and Mommy and Me in the Middle by Nina LaCour

Just Like a Mama by Alice Faye Duncan

MY BINDI

Written by Gita Varadarajan / Illustrated by Archana Sreenivasan
Grades 1–2 / Fiction / #OwnVoices

A Bit About the Book

Divya, a young Hindu girl, begins the brave work of showing up authentically at school. Old enough to understand the cultural and religious importance of wearing a bindi, Divya wants to wear one. Even her parents agree it is time to take this step. However, Divya fears the reactions of her classmates. With her parents' support and the strength she receives from the beautiful bindi she wears, Divya pushes past her fear not only by wearing the bindi to school but also by courageously explaining this aspect of her identity to her class.

SKILLS AND STANDARDS

Comprehension Skill:
Identify character's voice

CCSS: RL.1.3, RL.1.6 • SL.1.1.A, SL.1.3, SL.1.4, SL.1.6 • RL.2.3, RL.2.6 • SL.2.1.A, SL.2.3, SL.2.4, SL.2.6

Social Justice:
ID.K-2.3 (I know that all my group identities are part of me—but that I am always ALL me.)

CASEL:
Self-Awareness
• Integrate personal and social identities
• Identify personal, cultural, and linguistic assets
• Identify one's emotions

Identity

Strategy: Readers learn that some details in a story are specific pieces of information authors include to help us understand who is telling the story.

As You Read . . .
• Look closely at the way the author introduces the story.
• Notice both the details that are shared and the ways they are shared.
• Ask: *Who is telling the story?*

Places to Pause

During the initial reading of the book, pause after reading the first four pages and focus on the spread that shows Divya in the kitchen with her mother and father. Think aloud about the details we have learned in this beginning part of the story. Then, think aloud about who is telling the story. Ask: *What do the details tell us about the narrator's identity?* Finally, think about whether these details help us understand the problem in the story.

Circle Questions

Knowing who is telling a story helps us understand what the story really is about. Ask children: *What details show us who is narrating this story?*

Afterwards, invite children to reflect by saying: *Think about what your classmates said. Do you agree? If so, what other details can you add to support their answer? If you do not agree, what details support your answer about who the narrator is?*

Carryover Coaching

Use these additional prompts for one-on-one conferences.
• Reread the text slowly.
• Notice where details are shared in quotation marks and where they are shared without quotation marks.

- Ask: *Who is sharing the details in the story?*
- Say something about the narrator: *Most of the things I am learning about this story are/aren't in quotation marks and are mostly about (character). This makes me think the story is about (character).*

 ## Harm and Healing

Strategy: Readers determine whether actions, words, and other details in a book describe things that are taking place in the story or that are happening only in the character's imagination.

As You Read . . .
- Notice the actions, words, and details described.
- Decide if they are real things in the story or if they are imaginary.
- Ask: *Is this really happening to (character)?*
- Look for the characters' actions or talk.
- Ask: *How does (character) seem to know these details?*

Places to Pause
Pause after rereading the page on which Divya narrates Amma's belief that she should wear the bindi. Think aloud about whether the things that Divya describes are experiences she is having or possible experiences she worries about having. Take children through your thinking, naming the reason(s) you know Sam, Sally, and Sania have or have not said or done the things described.

Circle Questions
In the story, Divya tells how she feels and describes negative things her classmates say or do. Sometimes, characters experience negative things because they happen. Other times, they experience negative things not because they actually happened but because they understand how the world works and know that such things could happen. Ask children: *How can we tell what is real or what is imagined in the world the author creates?* As children share ideas, create a three-column chart on a sheet of chart paper. Label the columns: "Classmate," "Words or Actions," and "Real or Imagined." Ask children to retell each of Divya's classmate's actions or words and record the details they share under the appropriate column. Then, have children work with partners to determine whether each action is actually happening in the story or in Divya's mind, and note that on the chart.

Afterwards, invite children to reflect by saying: *Think about what your partner and classmates said. What do these tell us about the ways Divya may have learned about how people may treat others who are different from themselves in the real world?*

Carryover Coaching

Use these additional prompts for one-on-one conferences.

- Find a part that describes an action or where someone says something.
- Determine whether the action or dialogue is actually happening or imaginary.
- Think: *If this is not happening but could be happening, why is the author including it here?*
- Ask yourself: *Does this tell me something more about the character?*
- Think: *How does including events that are imaginary help me understand the story?*

SKILLS AND STANDARDS

Comprehension Skill:
Understand shades of meaning from words and phrases

CCSS: RL.1.1, RL.1.4 • SL.1.1.A, SL1.3, SL.1.4, SL.1.6 • L.1.5 • RL.2.1, RL.2.4 • SL.2.1A, SL.2.3, SL.2.4, SL.2.6 • L.2.5

Social Justice:
ID.K-2.1 (I know and like who I am and can talk about my family and myself and name some of my group identities.)

CASEL:
Self-Management
- Manage one's emotions
- Identify and use stress-management strategies
- Demonstrate personal and collective agency

Responsible Decision-Making
- Reflect on one's role to promote personal, family, and community well-being
- Evaluate personal, interpersonal, community, and institutional impacts

 Heartwork

Strategy: Readers can identify and explain how phrases that include *like* or *as* help them to better comprehend the text.

As You Read . . .

- Look for a phrase that includes the word *like* or *as* to describe something.
- Consider the ways the phrase helps you to visualize, or picture, the story in your mind.
- Think: *How would I see this part differently without this phrase?*

Places to Pause

Pause on the spread that shows Divya standing with a yellow-gold outline around her whole body. Have children close their eyes while you reread the words on the page. Encourage them to imagine themselves in Divya's place, acting out everything with their body or with their mind. Pause and let the room be silent after you read the last sentence. Then, ask children: *What does the expression, "slowly the words come cascading like a soft waterfall," make you see, feel, and hear?* Think aloud about how this helps you understand if Divya is, indeed, able to be brave.

Circle Questions

Turn to the page in which Divya is touching her bindi while the sun seems to be shining directly behind her head. Tell children: *Divya has taken the time to center herself—to close her eyes to everything that is outside of her, to listen to what she thinks, and to notice how these things make her feel. Now, she takes the additional step of touching the bindi, allowing all the parts of herself—her breath, her thoughts, her knowledge, her sight, and her sense of touch—to come together. At this point in the story and with all that we already know about Divya, what have we learned about her ability to be strong?*

Afterwards, invite children to reflect by saying: *Think about what your classmates shared. Do you have additional evidence to support something someone has stated?*

Carryover Coaching

Use these additional prompts for one-on-one conferences.

- Find a phrase that includes the words *like* or *as*.
- Cover the phrase with a finger or object and read the passage without it.
- Think: *Does not having that phrase change the way I understand this part of the story?*
- Uncover the phrase and reread the passage. Reflect on the way(s) the phrase changes the text and think about how this adds to the meaning of this part of the story.

🔁 Beyond the Book

One of the most moving parts of this book is a little sentence that could easily be overlooked. On the second page of printed text, the author shares that Divya is not the only Indian girl in her class: "Sania is Indian too." Through this we learn that not all Hindu girls may choose to wear a bindi. This brief but important part of the story can help children understand that there is diversity even within groups of people that seem the same. There are so many ways of being, so many different forms of diversity. The only possible way to understand this is to do what Divya did in this powerful story: Be brave enough to show up authentically.

Say to children: *We saw that Divya was very aware of the ways she was alike and different from other children in her class. We learned that this caused her to fear the way her classmates might respond to her based on a difference she was ready to share with them at school. What ways are we different that could be shared with others at school? How might sharing these differences help others feel safe about sharing more of who they are in school? What do we need to do to make sure our classroom is a space that allows everyone to be brave, like Divya?*

SKILLS AND STANDARDS

CASEL

Social Awareness

- Identify diverse social norms, including unjust ones
- Recognize situational demands and opportunities

Responsible Decision-Making

- Reflect on one's role to promote personal, family, and community well-being
- Evaluate personal, interpersonal, community, and institutional impacts
- Demonstrate curiosity and open-mindedness

A Few More Favorites

Bindu's Bindis
by Supriya Kelkar

The Boy & the Bindi
by Vivek Shraya

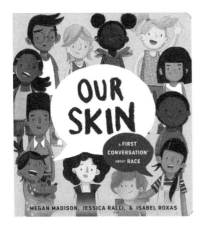

OUR SKIN: A FIRST CONVERSATION ABOUT RACE

Written by Megan Madison, Jessica Ralli, and Isabel Roxas
Grades 1–2 / Nonfiction / #OwnVoices

A Bit About the Book

This interactive, nonfiction text is a must-have book that can help teachers introduce the complex concepts of race and racism in child-friendly and accessible ways. The text teaches children about melanin and the sun, different identity groups, and how racism hurts. By balancing information and questions, the book creates spaces for children to engage, learn, think, and respond. The brightly colored illustrations depicting beautiful children in every shade bring a layer of joy and celebration to the text.

SKILLS AND STANDARDS

Comprehension Skill:
Analyze craft and structure

CCSS: RI.1.6 • SL.1.1., SL.1.2 • RI.2.6 • SL.2.1, SL.2.2

Social Justice:
ID.K-2.5 (I see that the way my family and I do things is both the same as and different from how other people do things, and I am interested in both.)

CASEL:
Self-Awareness
• Integrate personal and social identities
• Identify personal, cultural, and linguistic assets

Identity

Strategy: Readers of nonfiction know how to analyze the difference between the details we see in the pictures and the details we read in the words.

As You Read . . .

• Read through the pages.
• Look at the pictures and the words.
• Ask: *How are the pictures and the words the same and different?*

Places to Pause

Pause on the page in which the children play jump rope. Share what you notice about the picture, drawing attention to the children's actions—playing jump rope, riding a scooter, and playing with a dog. Then read the words aloud again. Model how you observe the differences between the words and the pictures. Turn the page and think aloud about what you notice in the picture of the family eating together. Then read the words and share what you notice about the similarities between the pictures and the words.

Circle Questions

Say to children: *We know that authors and illustrators both have a role. What can we learn as readers from the details the author writes and the details the illustrator draws? Ask yourself: "What can we as readers understand about the ways the messages work together?" Write down your reflections to share.*

Afterwards, invite children to reflect by saying: *Think to yourself: "Where else do we see words and illustrations working together to teach us something?"*

Carryover Coaching

Use these additional prompts for one-on-one conferences.

- Look closely at pictures across the pages.
- Tell the story using the pictures.
- Read the words across the pages.
- Compare the pictures and words.

 # Harm and Healing

Strategy: Readers of nonfiction learn about the author's purpose to support a message in a text.

As You Read . . .

- Look over the pictures and words of the story.
- Ask: *What do the pictures and words show about the book's message?*
- Make connections to the message and the author's purpose for writing this text.

Places to Pause

Pause after reading the two pages in which the author starts, "Skin color can't tell you much about what people are like. . . ." Think aloud about how you notice the characters have different skin colors and take part in different interests and activities. Model your reflection by saying how looking at someone from the outside doesn't tell us about who they are on the inside.

Circle Questions

Say to children: *We notice throughout the book that the author's message teaches us an important lesson: The way someone looks doesn't tell us about who they are, what they like, or their favorite foods/books. Think about what this message means to you. Write down your reflections. Share aloud.*

Afterwards, invite children to reflect by saying: *Think about a time when you met someone and got to know about them. Did the way they look affect what you thought of them before you got to know them? Share your reflections.*

Carryover Coaching

Use these additional prompts for one-on-one conferences.

- Look across the pages.
- Take note of the pictures and words.
- Make a connection to the message.
- Ask: *Why did the author write this book?*

SKILLS AND STANDARDS

Comprehension Skill:
Analyze author's purpose

CCSS: RI.1.4, RI.1.8 • SL.1.1, SL.1.3 • RI.2.4, RI.2.8 • SL.2.1, SL.2.3

Social Justice:
DI.K-2.3 (I know that all my group identities are part of me—but that I am always ALL me.)

CASEL:
Self-Awareness

- Integrate personal and social identities
- Identify personal, cultural, and linguistic assets
- Develop interests and a sense of purpose

Social Awareness

- Recognize strengths in others
- Take others' perspectives

SKILLS AND STANDARDS

Comprehension Skill:
Make inferences

CCSS: RI.1.1, RI.1.2, RI.1.3 • SL1.1.A, SL1.3, SL.1.4, SL.1.6 • RI.2.1, RI.2.2, RI.2.3 • SL2.1.A, SL.2.3, SL.2.4, SL.2.6

Social Justice:
AC.K-2.19 (I will speak up or do something if people are being unfair, even if my friends do not.)

CASEL:
Social Awareness
• Identify diverse social norms, including unjust ones
• Recognize situational demands and opportunities

 **Heartwork**

Strategy: Readers of nonfiction understand that we can learn more deeply about a topic by reading beyond what is on the pages.

As You Read . . .
• Think about and compare the ideas in the text.
• Determine which ideas seem more important than others.
• Ask: *What can I learn from this text?*

Places to Pause
Reread the last four pages of the text, beginning with the page that states: "Racism hurts and is always unfair." Put up a finger for each idea or action the author suggests readers do in response to racial injustice.

Circle Questions
Say to children: *Racism is such a big concept. In the book, the authors tell us a lot of ways we can work toward racial justice. Think about some of the things they suggested that you can do in school each day.*

Afterwards, invite children to reflect by saying: *We can work toward racial justice in many ways. Which of the ways the authors suggest feel like steps you have taken or steps you have seen your friends take?*

Carryover Coaching
Use these additional prompts for one-on-one conferences.
• Look across the pages.
• Think about the ideas or actions the authors suggest as ways to be racially just.
• Consider the actions you have done or seen others do.
• Determine if there are other actions you could add to the list.

 **Beyond the Book**

As we turn the pages of this book, we have the incredible opportunity to study the illustrations and see subjects with a variety of skin colors. To celebrate the children in your class, invite them to participate in a self-portrait project. You will need paper, mirrors, and skin-toned coloring supplies (crayons, markers, or colored pencils). Invite children to seat themselves in front of a mirror and look at themselves closely. Then have them begin to design, draw, and color themselves on a sheet of paper. Be sure to display children's self-portraits around the classroom to continue celebrating and honoring who they are!

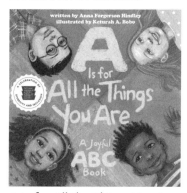

A child's self-portrait

A Few More Favorites

A Is for All the Things You Are
by Anna Forgerson Hindley

Skin Again
by bell hooks

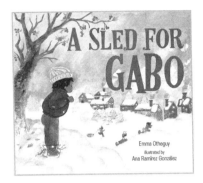

A SLED FOR GABO

Written by Emma Otheguy / Illustrated by Ana Ramírez González
Grades 1–2 / Fiction / #OwnVoices

A Bit About the Book

This story begins with Gabo looking out the window of his new home and watching the children from his new school play in the snow. Gabo wants nothing more than to join in on the fun. But with a hat that's too small, no boots or sled to be had, and no friends yet, he doesn't think it will happen. However, Gabo soon finds out that with some creative problem-solving, community, and a little bit of love, friendship and fun are just around the corner. *A Sled for Gabo* touches upon the challenges of poverty and the beauty of friendship in ways that are clear and tangible for even our youngest readers.

SKILLS AND STANDARDS

Comprehension Skill:
Infer about character

CCSS: RL.1.3, RL.1.7 • SL.1.1.A, SL.1.3, SL.1.4, SL.1.6 • RL.2.3, RL.2.7 • SL.2.1A, SL.2.3, SL.2.4, SL.2.6

Social Justice:
JU.K-2.14 (I know that life is easier for some people and harder for others and the reasons for that are not always fair.)

CASEL:
Social Awareness
• Understand and express gratitude

 ## Identity

Strategy: Readers learn about a character's identity by looking at what the character has and wants.

As You Read . . .
- Look closely at the character and his home.
- Notice what the character has, wants, and needs.
- Ask: *What does this help me understand about the character?*

Places to Pause

During the read-aloud, focus on the first few pages of the book and pause on the page that shows Gabo's mom helping him get ready to go outside. Pause at different points to name some of the things Gabo has that you may have as well; for example, a warm house, food to enjoy, and so on. Then, think about some of the things Gabo wants and why. Think aloud about how some of his "haves" and "wants" help you understand his desire for friends and fun, and how being open-minded around his wants helped him get those things.

Circle Questions

Say to children: *Even though sometimes not having something we want can seem like a problem, we can celebrate the things we do have and use them in all kinds of ways. Let's think about what Gabo did have in the story. We can look for things, people, or even animals. What good things did Gabo have in this story?*

Afterwards, invite children to reflect by saying: *Think about what your classmates said. What new ideas stand out most to you?*

Carryover Coaching

Use these additional prompts for one-on-one conferences.

- Look closely at the picture on a page.
- Point to things that the character has in his house.
- Think: *What doesn't he have? What else might he need?*
- Say something about the character: *Because he has/doesn't have . . ., I think . . .*

 ## Harm and Healing

Strategy: Readers look for the actions, words, and/or things that helped the character solve his problem.

As You Read . . .

- Notice some trouble that a character faces.
- Look for things that the character gets. Ask: *Did these help solve the problem?*
- Look for other characters' actions or words. Ask: *Did these help solve the problem, too?*

Places to Pause

Pause at the part in which Isa uses the tray Gabo received from Madrina as a sled. Talk children through your thinking—identify the problem as Gabo wanting to sled with friends but has neither a sled nor friends. Then think about the tray (a thing) as one part of the solution. Continue thinking aloud and notice the actions of Madrina (giving Gabo a gift), Sancho (running to Gabo and bringing Isa to him), and Isa (asking to play) as another part of the solution.

Circle Questions

Say to children: *In the story, Gabo met a new friend with whom to play in the snow. Let's think about all the people and things that helped Gabo make a friend.* Draw a web on chart paper. At the center of the web write: "Gabo wants a friend to play with, but he is shy." Then, as children share their ideas during the circle, write their thoughts on the web. (See sample on next page.)

Afterwards, invite children to reflect by saying: *Think about what your classmates said. What new ideas did they share that you hadn't thought of?*

Using this web, second graders shared ideas about who helped Gabo.

Carryover Coaching

Use these additional prompts for one-on-one conferences.

- Find a part in the book in which the character has a problem.
- Use the pictures. What is something he gets to help solve the problem?
- Find what characters say to one another to help solve the problem.
- Find what characters do to help solve of the problem.
- Put it together. What are all the ways the problem was solved?

SKILLS AND STANDARDS

Comprehension Skills:
Infer about character

CCSS: RL.1.3, RL.1.6 • SL.1.1.A, SL.1.3, SL.1.4, SL.1.6 • RL.2.3, RL.2.6 • SL.2.1.A, SL.2.3, SL.2.4, SL.2.6

Social Justice:
AC.K-2.18 (I will say something or tell an adult if someone is being hurtful, and will do my part to be kind even if I don't like something they say or do.)
AC.K-2.20 (I will join with classmates to make our classroom fair for everyone.)

CASEL:
Social Awareness
- Demonstrate empathy and compassion
- Show concern for the feelings of others
- Take others' perspectives
Relationship Skills
- Practice teamwork and collaborative problem-solving
- Resolve conflicts constructively

 **Heartwork**

Strategy: Readers observe how characters respond when another character is hurt.

As You Read . . .

- Look for a part in which a character feels bad.
- Watch for things that other characters around him do to help him or to be there for him.
- Think: *Why did the characters do that? What did they know about how the other character was feeling?*

Places to Pause

Pause on the page that shows Gabo's mom helping him find ways to go outside and play. Pause to think aloud about how we can tell that Gabo is upset. Then share how we can see that Mom understands how Gabo is feeling and is there for him. She reacts by saying they'll figure it out and then finds things around the house that will make it possible for Gabo to go play outside.

Circle Questions

Show children the page in which Gabo is outside pulling the candy out of his pockets. Say: *We know that Gabo was feeling sad here. If you were on the hill and saw Gabo feeling upset, what would you have done?*

Afterwards, invite children to reflect by saying: *Think about what your classmates shared. What new ideas did they share that taught you about what you could do to help someone who is feeling sad?*

Carryover Coaching

Use these additional prompts for one-on-one conferences.

- Find a sad/bad feeling in the book.
- Use the picture. What did a character do to help?
- Use the words. What did a character do to help?
- Put yourself in the main character's place. Ask yourself: *What am I feeling?*
- Put yourself in the place of the character who is helping. Ask: *Why did he or she do that?*

Beyond the Book

The beauty of *A Sled for Gabo* is found in the support of the community. From Señora Tobon sharing her mango to Madrina making a gift of a tray, we see this community connect and offer one another kindness in many forms. Bring the gift of community into the classroom by inviting children to brainstorm a way for their own community to offer one another kindness. This can be as complex or simple as you and your class decide to make it. You might decide to organize something as big as a schoolwide collection for those in need or something as small as a "kind words" exchange in the classroom. No matter what your class decides, be sure to highlight the gift of community and how, with the support of others, we can bring joy and comfort to many.

Invite children to brainstorm: *We saw that Gabo's neighbors offered help and kindness in many ways. Let's think of a way we can be just like Gabo's community. How might we help people in our school or class community? What can we do?*

SKILLS AND STANDARDS

CASEL
Responsible Decision-Making
- Reflect on one's role to promote personal, family, and community well-being
- Evaluate personal, interpersonal, community, and institutional impacts

A Few More Favorites

The Cot in the Living Room
by Hilda Eunice Burgos

Still a Family
by Brenda Reeves Sturgis

STELLA BRINGS THE FAMILY

Written by Miriam B. Schiffer / Illustrated by Holly Clifton-Brown
Grades K–2 / Fiction

A Bit About the Book

This heartfelt story about family is one that shines light on inclusivity and celebration. The story begins when Stella's teacher announces to the class that they will celebrate Mother's Day in school with a party, and the students will invite their moms to the celebration. Stella doesn't have a mom, but she has two dads. Feeling sad, worried, and stressed, Stella wonders how she will be able to celebrate Mother's Day if she does not have a mother she can bring to the party. With the support of her dads, close relatives, and classmates, Stella finds a way to celebrate with her loved ones that includes everyone!

SKILLS AND STANDARDS

Comprehension Skill:
Identify similarities and differences

CCSS: RL.K.1, RL.K.3, RL.K.7 • SL.K.1, SL.K.2 • RL.1.1, RL.1.3, RL.1.7 • SL.1.1, SL.1.2 • RL.2.1, RL.2.3, RL.2.7 • SL.2.1, SL.2.2

Social Justice:
ID.K-2.5 (I see that the way my family and I do things is both the same as and different from how other people do things, and I am interested in both.)
DI.K-2.7 (I can describe some ways that I am similar to and different from people who share my identities and those who have other identities.)

CASEL:
Self-Awareness
• Identify personal and social identities
Social Awareness
• Identify diverse social norms, including unjust ones

 **Identity**

Strategy: Readers learn that knowing our identities helps us discover how we are similar to and different from people who share our identities and those who have other identities.

As You Read . . .

• Look closely at the pages in which the author shows how the characters share identities.
• Notice how the characters are seen as the same and different.
• Ask: *What can we observe about identities and how characters are the same and different?*

Places to Pause

Pause on the pages in which Stella and her classmates ride their bikes and scooters as they leave at the end of the school day. Notice the children asking Stella how she does certain things without a mother. They continue to ask, "No mother?" Share Stella's responses to her classmates. Think aloud: *I can see that Stella shares a lot of similarities with her classmates as well as some differences.*

Circle Question

Say to children: *We see that Stella and her classmates share a lot of similarities. She and her classmates also share some differences. Share what the similarities and differences are.*

Afterwards, invite children to reflect by saying: *Think about our class. What are some of the ways we are the same? What are some of the ways we are different?*

Carryover Coaching

Use these additional prompts for one-on-one conferences.
- Look closely at the words between the characters.
- Think: *What is the same? What is different?*
- Say what is the same and what is different.

 ## Harm and Healing

Strategy: Readers can understand and relate to a character when her feelings change to worry.

As You Read . . .
- Notice how the character's words demonstrate her feelings of worry.
- Look for places where the character states her feelings of worry through words or actions.

Places to Pause

Pause at the part in which Stella learns about the Mother's Day celebration and begins to feel a sense of worry and stress. Think aloud: *What caused Stella to feel this way? How does this feeling affect the rest of her day at school?*

Circle Questions

Say to children: *We see that Stella feels worried because of a Mother's Day celebration at school. Let's think about how Stella feels and feel this with her.*

Afterwards, invite children to reflect by saying: *Share a time when you felt worried during the school day just as Stella did.*

SKILLS AND STANDARDS

Comprehension Skill:
Infer a character's feelings

CCSS: RL.K.1, RL.K.3, RL.K.7
• SL.K.1, SL.K.2 • RL.1.1, RL.1.3,
RL.1.7 • SL.1.1, SL.1.2 • RL.2.1,
RL.2.3, RL.2.7 • SL.2.1, SL.2.2

Social Justice:
DI.K-2.9 (I know everyone has feelings, and I want to get along with people who are similar to and different from me.)

CASEL:
Self-Awareness
- Identify one's emotions
- Link feelings, values, and thoughts
- Examine prejudices and biases

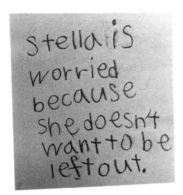

Children write about how Stella feels and why.

Carryover Coaching

Use these additional prompts for one-on-one conferences.

- Find a part in the story where you can relate to the character's feelings.
- Use the picture to explain how the character feels and connect with it.
- Share what caused the character to feel this way.

♥ Heartwork

Strategy: Readers observe how characters with different or similar identities can work together to find a solution.

As You Read . . .

- Look for moments when the characters work together to find a solution to a problem.
- Watch for moments when the characters support one another.
- Think: *How do the characters feel at this moment?*

Places to Pause

Pause on the page in which Stella comes home from school and shares about the Mother's Day celebration with her dads. Jonathan suggests that Stella should invite all the important people in her life, and her dads happily support this idea. Ask: *How does this solution help Stella?*

Circle Questions

Say to children: *Stella's family and friends thought of a different way to celebrate an important day that makes it more inclusive of everyone. How can we make sure we share celebrations with those who are different from and similar to ourselves? How might this have a positive impact on others?* Invite children to share their thoughts.

Afterwards, invite children to reflect by asking: *What ideas that were shared stand out to you most?*

Carryover Coaching

Use these additional prompts for one-on-one conferences.

- Find a moment in the story when a situation changed for the character.
- Use the picture and words to find when the characters worked together.
- Think: *What was the solution to the problem?*

 **Beyond the Book**

This wonderful story demonstrates a feeling of coming together—as families, school communities, and friends. *Stella Brings the Family* reminds us of the importance of inclusion, support for diverse experiences and perspectives, and leading as changemakers inside and outside of our classroom communities. Share stories and books about other changemakers with children. These leaders might be people within your community, your classroom, or in our world. Be sure to include stories of young changemakers. Then invite children to share some ways they want to be changemakers, and work together as a classroom community to put that plan into action!

A Few More Favorites

Mommy, Mama, and Me
by Lesléa Newman

When Aidan Became a Brother
by Kyle Lukoff

UNDER MY HIJAB

Written by Hena Khan / Illustrated by Aaliya Jaleel
Grades K–2 / Fiction / #OwnVoices

A Bit About the Book

This inspirational and empowering picture book introduces readers to hijabs. Through words and illustrations, we see special moments and memories Muslim women and girls celebrate when wearing the hijab in their daily lives. Read on to learn about the women in the main character's life and the strength and bond in each of her relationships.

SKILLS AND STANDARDS

Comprehension Skill:
Infer character identity

CCSS: RL.K.1, RL.K.3, RL.K.7
• SL.K.1, SL.K.2 • RL.1.1, RL.1.3, RL.1.7 • SL.1.1, SL.1.2 • RL.2.1, RL.2.3, RL.2.7 • SL.2.1, SL.2.2

Social Justice:
ID.K-2.2 (I can talk about interesting and healthy ways that some people who share my group identities live their lives.)

CASEL:
Self-Awareness
• Integrate personal and social identities
• Identify personal, cultural, and linguistic assets

Identity

Strategy: Readers learn about a character's identity through the activities she engages in and the people who surround her.

As You Read . . .
• Look closely at the pictures.
• Notice the actions the character takes.
• Ask: *What can we learn about the character's identity from the actions she takes?*

Places to Pause

Pause on the first few pages in which the main character introduces us to women with whom she is close. We learn about her grandmother, her mother, and her aunt. Notice the actions each character engages in over the pages. Ask children: *What does this tell us about each character's identity?* Create an identity chart for one of the characters—observe her hobbies, actions, and possibly physical or cultural markers.

Circle Questions

Say to children: *We notice in the story that each character takes a different action throughout the pages. Think about what this says about people and their identities. We might find ourselves relating to the characters in the book in different ways. How can you relate your actions to your identity? What are some of the things you do that are a part of your identity?*

Afterwards, invite children to reflect by asking: *What did someone share that helped you see something in a brand-new way?*

> Character Identity
> - loves her family
> - enjoys hiking
> - likes to have slumber parties with friends
> - sisters - big/little sister time
> - girl scout, loves to cook

Charting our reflections on character identity from *Under My Hijab*

Carryover Coaching

Use these additional prompts for one-on-one conferences.

- Look closely at the pictures.
- Point to a character's actions.
- Think: *What does this say about the character's identities?*

 ## Harm and Healing

Strategy: Readers know we can learn about relationships through the characters and their interactions.

As You Read . . .

- Notice the characters' interactions.
- Look at what the characters say to one another.
- Look at the characters' expressions.

Places to Pause

Pause at the part in which the main character is at a picnic with all of the important women in her life. Ask children: *What do you notice about the connection the main character has to each of these characters through her interactions in the story?* Share how the main character feels inspired by these women and the relationships she has with them.

Circle Questions

Ask children: *Why do you think the main character feels inspired?* Have them think about a time when they have felt that way through a relationship they have with someone close to them. Invite children to share why they feel inspired or supported by that person.

SKILLS AND STANDARDS

Comprehension Skill: Infer about characters' relationships

CCSS: RL.K.1, RL.K.3, RL.K.7, SL.K.1, SL.K.2 • RL.1.1, RL.1.3, RL.1.7 • SL.1.1, SL.1.2 • RL.2.1, RL.2.3, RL.2.7 • SL.2.1, SL.2.2

Social Justice:
ID.K-2.1 (I know and like who I am and can talk about my family and myself and name some of my group identities.)

CASEL:
Social Awareness
- Recognize strengths in others
- Understand and express gratitude
Relationship Skills
- Develop positive relationships

Afterwards, invite children to reflect by asking: *What did someone share that made you think "Me, too!"?*

Carryover Coaching
Use these additional prompts for one-on-one conferences.
- Find a part in which the characters interact with one another.
- Use the picture to describe the characters' feelings.
- Ask: *What do their interactions tell us about the characters?*

SKILLS AND STANDARDS

Comprehension Skill:
Identify cause and effect

CCSS: RL.K.1, RL.K.3, RL.K.7
• SL.K.1, SL.K.2 • RL.1.1, RL.1.3, RL.1.7 • SL.1.1, SL.1.2 • RL.2.1, RL.2.3, RL.2.7 • SL.2.1, SL.2.2

Social Justice:
DI.K-2.6 (I like being around people who are like me and different from me, and I can be friendly to everyone.)

CASEL:
Self-Awareness
• Integrate personal and social identities
• Identify personal, cultural, and linguistic assets
• Develop interests and a sense of purpose

♥ Heartwork

Strategy: Readers watch how a character changes throughout a story.

As You Read . . .
- Look for ways the character interacts with others.
- Watch for how the character changes from the beginning to the end.
- Think: *How did the character change throughout the story?*

Places to Pause
Pause on the last page of the story. Notice the main character putting on her own hijab and adding some decoration to it. Think aloud: *What experiences has the character gone through in this story?* Ask children: *How has the character changed? What caused this change for her?*

Circle Questions
Say to children: *We notice the character puts on her hijab at the end of the story. Her expression and words describe her feelings. Share how you think the character feels at this point and what events throughout the story influenced this change for her.*

Afterwards, invite children to reflect by asking: *What did someone share that you thought about already? What did someone share that you hadn't thought of yet?*

Carryover Coaching
Use these additional prompts for one-on-one conferences.
- Find a picture that shows the character at the beginning of the story and another that shows the character at the end.
- Ask: *What is different about the character? What is the same?*
- Feel what the character is feeling at the end of the story.

 **Beyond the Book**

This story introduces us to the empowering experience and celebration for Muslim women in their choice to wear a hijab. Throughout the book, we see the main character looking up to the women in her life and her relationships with each of them.

Have children brainstorm someone in their lives whom they look up to, who is a positive influence for them, or whom they aspire to be like. Encourage them to share about the person with the class. Then invite them to write a letter to that special person. The letter can include details of their gratitude to that person, how they have felt inspired by that individual, or why they look up to them. Children can then choose to share their letter with that special someone.

SKILLS AND STANDARDS

CASEL
Social Awareness
• Recognize strengths in others
• Understand and express gratitude

A Few More Favorites

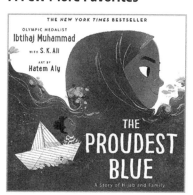

The Proudest Blue
by Ibtihaj Muhammad

Lailah's Lunchbox
by Reem Faruqi

ZONIA'S RAIN FOREST
Written and illustrated by Juana Martinez-Neal
Grades K–2 / Fiction / #OwnVoices

A Bit About the Book

This beautifully illustrated book offers readers a window into the world within the Peruvian Amazon. Told from the perspective of Zonia, a sweet and energetic little girl, we see the joys and wonders of the natural world, as well as the worry and hurt brought by deforestation. In addition to Zonia's heartfelt story, the last few pages deepen readers' understanding of the Ashaninka people who inhabit the land, the wildlife they share it with, and the threats and harm that human choices have caused to all who live there as well as to the planet itself.

SKILLS AND STANDARDS

Comprehension Skill:
Infer about character

CCSS: RL.K.2, RL.K.3 • SL.K.1.A–B, SL.K.2, SL.K.6 • RL.1.2, RL.1.3 • SL.1.1.A, SL.1.2, SL.1.6 • RL.2.2, RL.2.3 • SL.2.1.A, SL.2.2, SL.2.6

Social Justice
DI.K-2.7 (I can describe some ways that I am similar to and different from people who share my identities and those who have other identities.)
DI.K-2.9 (I know everyone has feelings, and I want to get along with people who are similar to and different from me.)

CASEL
Self-Awareness
• Recognize strengths in others

 **Identity**

Strategy: Readers notice ways that the character's identities are different from our own.

As You Read . . .

- Pause to list all that we are learning about the character's identities.
- Think about things that make this character's life different from our own.
- Name things that we learn or can appreciate about how this character lives differently.

Places to Pause

Pause on the page that shows Zonia nose to nose with a coati. Talk about what you have seen of her identities so far. You might point out things such as her home, her being indigenous, or her play from the first few pages. Explicitly name things about Zonia and her life that are different from your own. Then, share some of the differences that you appreciate about her and her life. (For example: She has fun with wild animals. She plays in a rain forest.)

Circle Questions

Say to children: *Think about Zonia and her world. What was different and interesting about her or her life?*

Afterwards, invite children to reflect by asking: *What do you appreciate about Zonia's life based on what your friends shared in the circle?*

Carryover Coaching

Use these additional prompts for one-on-one conferences.

- Use the pictures and words to think about the character.
- Name what you know about the character's identities. Use what she looks like, what she does, and what we see around her.
- Ask yourself: *What makes her different from me?*
- List things you learned or like about your differences.

 ## Harm and Healing

Strategy: Readers think about messages from books they read by asking questions that begin with *who, how,* or *why.*

As You Read . . .
- Name the problem.
- Ask: *Who is affected by this? How does it affect them? Why are they affected?*
- Based on these questions, think about a message we may learn from the book.

Places to Pause

On the page that shows Zonia talking to her mother about the destroyed forest, take a few moments to think aloud. For this modeling opportunity, focus on "who" and "how" questions: *Who is being affected by the cutting down of the trees? How is it hurting them?* Share some of your thoughts based on the questions you asked.

Circle Questions

Read aloud the fact pages at the end of the book. Say to children: *Now that we know a bit more about what is happening to the rain forests, what message do you think this book is sending?*

Afterwards, invite children to reflect by asking: *What new ideas did your friends share that you hadn't thought about?*

SKILLS AND STANDARDS

Comprehension Skill:
Ask questions

CCSS: RL.K.1, RL.K.3 • SL.K.1.A–B, SL.K.2., SL.K.6 • RL.1.1, RL.1.3 • SL.1.A, SL.1.2, SL.1.6 • RL.2.1, RL.2.3 • SL.2.1.A, SL.2.2, SL.2.6

Social Justice:
JU.K-2.14 (I know that life is easier for some people and harder for others and the reasons for that are not always fair.)

CASEL:
Responsible Decision-Making
- Anticipate and evaluate the consequences of one's actions
- Demonstrate curiosity and open-mindedness

Kindergartners offer ideas during a circle share.

Carryover Coaching

Use these additional prompts for one-on-one conferences.

- Look for a place in the book in which the character becomes upset.
- Use the pictures to see who is affected by the problem.
- Think: *What will this do to those who are affected?*
- Think about questions you have about the problem.
- Try to use the book to help you answer these questions.

SKILLS AND STANDARDS

Comprehension Skill:
Make inferences

CCSS: RL.K.3 • SL.K.1.A–B, SL.1.2, SL.1.6 • RL.1.3 • SL.1.1.A, SL.1.2, SL.1.6 • RL.2.3 • SL.2.1.A, SL.2.2, SL.2.6

Social Justice:
JU.K-2.12 (I know when people are treated unfairly.)
JU.K-2.14 (I know that life is easier for some people and harder for others and the reasons for that are not always fair.)

CASEL:
Social Awareness
- Show concern for the feelings of others
Relationship Skill
- Stand up for the rights of others

♥ Heartwork

Strategy: Readers notice when something seems unfair.

As You Read . . .

- Stop when you notice a problem in the text.
- Ask: *Is there something unfair about this?*
- Think about how the problem is unfair and who it hurts.

Places to Pause

Pause on the page that shows Zonia running into the area that has all the cut-down trees. Pause to name the problem for children. Think aloud about how this seems unfair to the community and to the animals affected by this. Share how this problem takes away parts of their home.

Circle Questions

Say to children: *We know that what is happening in Zonia's rain forest feels unfair. Let's think about times when we've experienced something unfair, too. Tell something that happened to you that was unfair and how it made you feel. That will help us understand how Zonia must feel.*

Afterwards, invite children to reflect by asking: *What do you think about fairness now that you have heard your friends' stories?*

Carryover Coaching

Use these additional prompts for one-on-one conferences.

- Stop when the character seems upset.
- Think about what is happening. Ask: *Is that fair? Why or why not?*
- Find the characters who feel hurt. Ask: *How is this unfair to them? How did it hurt them?*

 **Beyond the Book**

Sometimes problems require someone else's help. It is important to know how to ask others how we can help or support them. Having the language to offer support is a key component in social and emotional learning. During the session, teach children that when they see someone hurting, they can ask if that person needs help. Brainstorm a sentence that offers them helpful language. For example: "I see you're upset. How can I help?" To extend this into literacy work, take children's ideas and engage in an interactive writing exercise to create a sign to hang up in the classroom.

Say to children: *In the story, Zonia knows that the forest is asking for help and that we all need to do something. It's important for us to notice when someone needs help and how to ask them what we can do. Let's imagine that we see a friend crying or looking sad and think of some things we can say to find out how we can help. We'll write our ideas down so we can remember what to say when that happens in our classroom.*

SKILLS AND STANDARDS

CASEL
Relationship Skills
• Seek or offer support and help when needed
• Stand up for the rights of others

A Few More Favorites

The Thing About Bees
by Shabazz Larkin

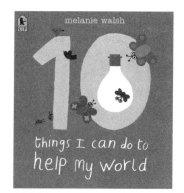

10 Things I Can Do to Help My World
by Melanie Walsh

THE FINAL PART

A trait many of us educators share is our love of books. We know that if we happen across a bookstore in our travels, we will be pulled into its doors. We get lost in the children's section for an eternity. Hours later, we emerge, arms loaded with new adventures for our students to get lost in, too. This is an absolute truth for us.

So, as you can imagine, narrowing down the stories to include in this resource was no easy task. The more covers we cracked open and explored, the more books we fell in love with. We wish we could have offered you even more stories. We also know that as this resource sits in your hands, more and more brand-new future favorites will fill up bookstore shelves.

The good news: The lenses and lessons can go beyond the books we've shared here. You can transfer the strategies to other texts. The thinking can and should be carried away from the mentor texts and into the books that live in our students' independent reading baggies and choice texts. So feel free to continue shopping for other books!

Bringing the Reading Lenses to the Bookstore

When seeking books for primary classrooms, we often use a mental checklist to ensure that the books we offer will be engaging, authentic, and allow children to pretend themselves into the story. While we don't walk around bookstores with a checklist in hand, here are a few things to look for as you explore the shelves.

- #OwnVoices authors
- Colorful and engaging artwork
- Clear images of facial expressions and expressive bodies
- Characters with identities that match those of children (and adults) in your classroom
- Characters with identities that offer a peek into someone else's world
- Celebrations that honor different identities
- Challenges that children can understand
- Language variety: Ways that different identity groups express themselves
- Authenticity (avoid books with tokenized or stereotypical characters)

Why We Prioritized #OwnVoices

On September 6, 2015, Corinne Duyvis created and defined #OwnVoices, a hashtag that became a movement. In a tweet, she defined #OwnVoices as texts "about diverse characters written by authors from that same diverse group" (2015). In the thread that followed, she added more clarity by stating the intent is "to lift up those who are often ignored" and to represent "all kinds of marginalized groups." Subsequently, the movement grew, and the hashtag was co-opted by the publishing industry, who turned it into a catch-all marketing phrase that eventually blurred its original meaning and intent. Although this resulted in the organization We Need Diverse Books deciding to cease use of the term, we have chosen to center #OwnVoices—as it was originally intended—in our work.

Picture books contain two messages—one by the author and one by the illustrator. Because of this, we have expanded the definition of #OwnVoices to include books in which either the author or illustrator or both hold the marginalized status of the main character(s). The book shopping "checklist" we presented earlier, as well as the content of our book, hopefully presents our belief that it is important to center historically and/or culturally marginalized voices in the texts we use to teach—not just the ones we add to the classroom library. Furthermore, we aspire to ensure each text we select satisfies two critical criteria put forth by educator Laura Jiménez:

- "It must be an authentic representation that shows marginalized individuals as whole people, living complex lives that do not adhere to the dominant White narrative."
- "It must push back against biased narratives of the community." (Jiménez, 2021).

Creating Your Own Strategies

One goal of this resource is to give teachers a few ready-to-go lessons to have at their fingertips. We know what it is like to have so much to plan and not enough time to plan it! However, we don't believe that you have to teach the strategies and lessons we've provided exactly as we've laid them out or with the mentor texts we've selected. We hope that you will come up with your own authentic strategies for your teaching as well. Unpacking your own process will allow you to use the texts we've centered in new ways. A fun and fruitful way to create your own strategies is to spy on yourself as a reader and notice how your own brain works to comprehend and think about the text. If you're planning to create your own strategies, here's a mini guide to help you bring your thinking process to life for your readers.

A Strategy for Strategy Making
1. Choose a skill and practice doing it in your mentor text (e.g., identify a character trait).
2. Ask yourself: *How did I just do that? What did I look at, ask myself, or think about?*
3. Put your process into a few actionable steps.

If you are carrying a strategy into another text, go back to the steps. Think about a place in the new book that would fit the strategy. Then, bring yourself through the steps to plan out your modeling and think-aloud for children.

Circles for Change in Your School Community

Our invitation with the stories and lessons in this resource is to shift our practice to make it student-centered. In doing so, we aim to reach all individuals by creating a space and experience to feel seen, heard, and understood. We extend our work to take the necessary steps toward identity, healing, and heartwork. This book serves as an invitation for educators, children, and the community alike. We know these conversations are crucial. Our next questions are: *How do we begin? How do we hear from the voices that have not been heard yet?*

Throughout this book, we present numerous examples of restorative practices and circle conversations to engage in with children. We can utilize the same practices with adults as well. Our adult-to-adult conversations might be between groups of educators, between educators and parents, or among educators and PTO leadership. Ultimately, we might have these conversations when we find ourselves in an opportune position to engage with any other stakeholder within our educational institutions. Among colleagues, these circle conversations can extend to faculty meetings, professional learning communities (PLCs), and collaborative partnerships across grade levels, subject matters, districts, and states. Among stakeholders, these conversations can occur within board of education meetings, parent presentations, and back-to-school nights. We can use the design and implementation of circle conversations or book clubs to guide and support this work together.

We recognize that sometimes there are a very limited number of opportunities, if any, for this type of connection and conversation. We acknowledge that spaces defined by a culture of toxicity, resistance, and isolation do exist. We also realize that many of us might feel alone in this work. For those of us educators who are seeking a community of partners and collaborators, there fortunately exists an extensive support system within larger educational groups. You can find these through social media, educational blogs, and collaborative teaching institutions, to name just a few. We want to assure you that you don't have to feel alone in your work with this text and that there are always partnerships available for support and collaboration.

Taking a moment to honor and recognize the various stages you might find yourself in with this work, we want to share some "go-to" resources you might use when starting up the conversation with stakeholders, regardless of where you might be on this path.

- "The 60-Second Confrontation Model" from *Fierce Conversations,* by Susan Scott (https://resources.finalsite.net/images/v1571246492/psesdorg/flklvf6unbeqi0muplzc/Confrontation-Model-Fierce-Conversation.pdf)
- *Let's Talk!* from Learning for Justice (https://www.learningforjustice.org/magazine/publications/lets-talk)
- Knoster Model for Managing Complex Change (https://blog.edsmart.com/managing-change-in-schools-a-helpful-framework)

NOTES FROM THE AUTHORS

A Note From Dana

As a White, cisgendar female, my childhood was full of storybook characters who looked like me. I befriended Beverly Cleary's Ramona and considered myself one of the girls from The Baby-Sitters Club series. Then, as I got a bit older, Judy Blume's Margaret and Katherine taught me important lessons about growing up and first loves. Belonging and mirrors were not a problem for me, as everywhere I looked I found reflections of myself on library shelves. So, why do I still feel like I missed something vital in my early reading life? I've come to believe that it is because while my childhood had wall-to-wall mirroring, there wasn't a single window to be found. The stories I loved, and continue to love, were wonderful. But they didn't offer me opportunities to see worlds, experiences, and beautiful people who didn't look like me, and collectively sent a hidden message of white superiority that I am continuously working to unlearn.

I don't blame my teachers. I was lucky to have had many wonderful educators who gave love freely and were always looking to create community. I do, however, acknowledge that our educational community is and has been well aware of how the lack of representation in our classroom libraries "others" students and sends messages that they don't belong, while also creating missed opportunities to learn about one another.

This is what pushed me to collaborate and write this book with my two amazing coauthors, Jigisha Vyas and Keisha Smith-Carrington. I am deeply grateful for their mentorship and the ways that this writing has moved me forward on my own journey toward anti-biased and antiracist teaching practices. This particular journey will be lifelong.

Contributing to this book is one step along the way. My mentor and colleague Gravity Goldberg often says that we write what we need to learn and hear. This feels especially true for me in coauthoring this project. I hope that this resource is what you needed as well, and that it can be one part of your learning journey as we move forward together to create classrooms that both center our shared humanity and celebrate the beauty of our unique identities.

A Note From Keisha

Most educators can easily name one or more books that were their favorite(s) when they were children. I cannot. Instead of one or more books, I can name the context in which books were read to me as my earliest memories of reading. In my mind, it was an every-night occurrence, although I am pretty sure this is a child's recollection. I know for a fact that the readings involved my maternal grandmother, Shirley.

Grandma Shirley and my mom (Sheila Smith) each worked separate shifts at the post office. As a manager, my grandmother worked days. This meant that most nights I was at my grandmother's house at bedtime. After tucking me in bed, she would pull from a collection of books and read to me with perfect prosody. I don't know who enjoyed this routine more—her or me. I remember warmth. I remember laughter. I remember being centered.

As an adult, I do not remember ever having any character in any of the books we read reflect me. It wasn't until I was a mother developing my children's library of bedtime and other-time readings that I discovered the works of authors like Eloise Greenfield. I do not have enough space to share the effect of seeing my name—albeit with another spelling—in her book *My Doll, Keshia*. But that feeling, combined with the effect of seeing Jan Gilchrist's illustrations of brown-skinned girls rocking Afro puffs, compelled me to include representation and cultural relevance in my home and classroom libraries.

My experiences as a reader, mother, and teacher have allowed me to witness the impact of texts on children who hold many identities. Being able to bring these older experiences and the more recent learning I've done with colleagues in my professional home into this work with Dana and Jigisha has been a wonderful experience. I am grateful for the learning community we've formed and am excited about the many educators who will join us in bringing this work to more children.

A Note From Jigisha

Growing up as a little Brown girl who identifies as Indian American and as a child of immigrants, I recall running my fingers across the spines of books on the shelves in my elementary school's library. My eyes were constantly searching for a book that would intrigue and engage my young mind and heart. As a child, I was drawn to adventure. Having been inspired by stories of trailblazing women such as Amelia Earhart, I yearned to read stories that featured characters who were driven by their curiosities and dreams.

I remember the day I discovered and developed an interest in reading the Cam Jansen series. The books feature a fifth-grade female protagonist with photographic memory who embarks on numerous adventures with her best friend to solve a slew of mysteries. I would read through the pages in class and then go on adventures with my friends after school to solve our own versions of "mysteries." One of our favorites included the use of invisible ink and a "missing" stuffed Dalmatian dog.

I vividly recall the moment I found myself observing the cover of the Cam Jansen books. They featured a little White girl with red hair, who looked very similar to all the other characters I had seen in the books that lined our library's shelves. I would search through the stories to see if there were any books with characters who looked like me, had a name like mine, or celebrated the same holidays as me. I didn't know it then, but I would spend the next 20 years waiting to discover a children's book in which I could finally see myself. I'd wait 20 years for little Brown girls everywhere to finally be seen.

My 2-year-old niece, Mia, is bright, joyful, and has a deep love for reading. She lights up our world! She has engaged with books and stories since she was only a few weeks old. Recently, Mia and I were immersed in reading the book *My Bindi,* by Gita Varadarajan. This heartwarming story is about a little Brown girl named Divya and her journey to finding empowerment and pride in her Indian American heritage, particularly in finding strength and love in her family as she proudly wears her *bindi.* As we turned the pages of the story, Mia would point to Divya's character and happily say "Mia" on each single page. My heart was so full from watching my niece be able to see herself in this story and feel seen. We then proceeded to decorate ourselves with elaborate *bindis* and celebrate the beauty of the moment.

I am confident that readers can share this experience across all reading spaces with the lessons and stories featured in this resource. Having the fortunate opportunity to coauthor this book with Dana and Keisha, I feel a deep and immense gratitude and have a great sense of hope and joy for these special moments to happen for young hearts and minds everywhere.

ACKNOWLEDGMENTS

From Dana

Every choice we make means saying yes to some things and saying no to others. Every time I said yes to making space for writing, I may have been saying no to watching one of my sons' hockey games or swim meets, cuddling up on the couch sandwiched between beautiful boys to watch a favorite show, or being the caregiver in charge of that night's dinner or homework help. Of course, there were many times when the writing got a no and my family got the yes, but my contributions to this project wouldn't have been possible without the constant understanding, support, and encouragement of my amazing partner in life, Yuma Clark, and my two wonderful children, John and Tommy. Yuma, you are the best human I know and will forever be the best choice of my life. John and Tommy, you are my heart. Writing this has been in part to make sure that children like you see themselves and their histories in their classroom experiences. Thank you for giving me the best job of my life, being your mother. And thank you to all my family and friends who may have seen a bit less of me but were there to celebrate good days and hold space and support for me on the hard ones.

In addition to home family support, my educational family has been instrumental from the beginning. Thank you to my GG LLC teammates—Gravity Goldberg, Sarah Fiedeldey, Pam Koutrakos, Heather Frank, Margy Leininger, Brianne Annitti, Christy Curran, Lily Howard Scott, Laura Sarsten, and Julie Mc Auley. Your influence lives in everything I do. To Patty McGee, Steve Fiedeldey, and Wendy Murray, without you this version of the book would still be buried deep in Google Drive. Thank you for your inspiration and support. I love you all. Thank you to my dear friends at The Curious Reader in Glen Rock, New Jersey. When it comes to helping me find new books to bring into my teaching and my home, you are my people. Of course, I also want to thank all the inspirational educators in my partner schools. I am grateful to learn with and from all of you. A special thanks goes out to Washingtonville's Ashley Scelia, Debra Zupko, Kara Haney, and Jen Burke and Paramus's Christina Rizzo, who tested out lessons and opened up their classrooms as playful learning spaces. Last but not least, to my Wednesday night kiddos—Nicco, Sylvi, Elenor, and Samantha, and their families. Our little crew not only helped us refine some of our lessons but your light and the laughter we shared brought so much joy into my world.

One last thank you goes out to a whole different family—my writing friends. A great big thank you to the folks at Teach Write with Jennifer Laffin. Many pages were born during Time to Write sessions. And an especially big dollop of love to my feedback fam—Kerry Chapman, Tracy Vogelgesang, and Michelle Sheehan. You ladies have been so much more than writing support. Thank you for your honest feedback, but mostly for your friendship. I adore you.

From Keisha

I would not be the reader I am today if it weren't for my Grandma Shirley, who modeled being a voracious reader. She took her last breath the season before I agreed to write this resource and would have been extremely excited and proud that her actions contributed to me becoming an author.

In addition to my maternal grandmother, I am grateful for my adult-ren, Avey and Ashby. Each of them continues to affect the ways I look at texts. Each of them still impacts my social and emotional development. Each of them helped me, during a very difficult year, to persist through the end of my contributions to this book.

In my current professional home, there are folks whose approaches to working with children have greatly affected my practice over the last four years. These include my teammates in leading the district's equity learning (Thomas Foley, Dawn Henderson, Liz Lien, Patty Manhart, and Jen Simon) and Gita Varadarajan, a thought partner always opening her classroom as a space in which we help each other hone skills related to this book.

Beyond my professional home, there are the visionary leaders of the Institute for Racial Equity in Literacy (IREL)—Dr. Sonja Cherry-Paul and Tricia Ebarvia—and the many folks in the community they cultivate with facilitators (Aeriale, Anna, Michelle, Min, Tiana, and many more), participants (like Clare, who expanded my thinking on the intersectional use of picture books by introducing me to her work with Lynsey, Franki, and Dr. Jiménez), and keynote speakers (like Dr. Sealey-Ruiz, whose Racial Literacy Development Theory and loving ways of being now ground my praxis).

From Jigisha

Throughout my life, my mother's wisdom has echoed in my mind and has remained in my heart. She taught me to always allow myself to be open to life's unfoldings and invitations. In those moments when it feels like a number of doors are closing, there is purpose and intention leading you to the ones that will be open for you. These words have led me to have transformative experiences and have manifested a deep sense of gratitude for each singular moment.

My parents, Kishor and Kokila, have been the guiding lights throughout my life. Leaving their home country of India, my parents immigrated to the United States in their late 20s. They left behind their families, homes, and a familiar world for one that is new, unfamiliar, exciting, and different, and they navigated the journey of building their home and their lives here. The leaps they took, the experiences they endured, the trials and errors they navigated were all centered on creating opportunity for their children. They made personal sacrifices, including overnight shifts, numerous jobs, discontinuing a pursuit to further their careers, and not spending money on themselves to save for their children's violin lessons, dance classes, and basketball camps. Their time, love, energy, and sacrifices have made it possible for doors to open for me. Their wisdom—a collection of messages and support that is both grounding and uplifting; a combination of their stories and those of my grandparents, great-grandparents, and ancestors; and a wonderful mix of encouragement and enlightenment—continues to transform my life daily and will shine its light on the generations to come. To my parents—who are my protectors, my guardians, my lifelong teachers, and my friends—words are not enough to express my love, gratitude, and appreciation for you both.

To my husband, Ashish—this project could not have been possible without you. Your unwavering love, support, and encouragement have made this dream a reality for me. I am grateful for all the moments you have been my thinking partner, my sounding board, and the person who brings laughter and light into my life, especially after some of the longer days of writing. You are my best friend, the answer to a thousand prayers, and a constant supporter of my wildest dreams. Thank you for always encouraging me and reminding me about the purpose and intention of this work, for grounding me in the reasons I was called to be an educator, and for being my inspiration to leave this world a little bit better than we found it.

Every encounter and interaction leave us with a seed that is the foundation of learning and growth. I am so deeply thankful to my family and friends, who have shared stories, smiles, laughter, and tears as we talked about our own personal moments when we felt truly understood. Each of you is an inspiration for this book. And here's a final note of gratitude for the moments of connection with all my students, my teachers, and my fellow educators: Thank you for reminding me each day that we cannot stop transforming our world for children to feel seen, heard, and safe; for students to feel cared for, loved, and supported; and for students to have an infinite number of doors open for them.

From All of Us
Schools
This book truly could not have come to life until we were able to move the work from the ideas that existed in our minds into real-life lesson work in classrooms with little humans. There are so many awesome educators who helped us put theories into practice and refine our ideas. Special thanks go out to the leaders of all our partner schools across New York and New Jersey. Specifically, thank you to Paramus Public Schools, Princeton Public Schools, Washingtonville Central School District, and Wyckoff Public Schools. And to the amazing teachers who tried out the work and opened their hearts and their classrooms to us—Jennifer Burke, Ashley Scelia, Debra Zupko, and Christina Rizzo—we love you and are eternally grateful for your partnership.

Scholastic
AND OF COURSE . . . a giant thank you to the folks at Scholastic. To our fabulous editor, Maria L. Chang, we are eternally grateful for your flexibility and love, as well as for offering thoughtful and generous feedback with a smile. To Trent Hanover, for answering every question and creating comfort in our partnership. To Tannaz Fassihi, we are so grateful to partner with you in making the cover everything we could have hoped for and more. To Shelley Griffin and Samantha Unger, thank you for hearing us speak about our work and sharing it with a larger audience. To Bobby McCabe, we are so grateful and awed by the ways that you design tools to perfectly match our team's vision. To Annie Stubbs and Jacqueline Biltucci, thank you for helping us launch our stories and share our book on a broader scale. To Tara Welty, for believing in and supporting our work. And to Michelle Kim, for seeing our vision and bringing life to our ideas on the page. Thank you to the Scholastic team for your support and for your belief in us and this book.

RESOURCES

Achor, S. (2011). *The happiness advantage: The seven principles that fuel success and performance at work.* Virgin.

Achor, S. (2018). *Big potential.* Crown.

Ahmed, S. K. (2018). *Being the change: Lessons and strategies to teach social comprehension.* Heinemann.

Arnsten, A. F. (2015). "Stress weakens prefrontal networks: Molecular insults to higher cognition." *Nature Neuroscience, 18*(10), 1376.

Bidol, P. A. (1972). *Developing new perspectives on race: An innovative multi-media social studies curriculum in racism awareness for the secondary level.* New Perspectives on Race.

Bishop, R. S. (1990). "Mirrors, windows, and sliding glass doors." In H. Moir (Ed.), *Collected perspectives: Choosing and using books for the classroom, 6*(3). Christopher-Gordon Publishers

Brackett, M. A. (2020). *Permission to feel: The power of emotional intelligence to achieve well-being and success.* Celadon Books.

Brown, B. (2012). *Listening to shame.* TED Talks. Retrieved March 28, 2022, from https://www.ted.com/talks/brene_brown_listening_to_shame?language=en

Brown, B. (2015). *Daring greatly: How the courage to be vulnerable transforms the way we live, love, parent, and lead.* Avery.

Brown, B. (2022). *Atlas of the heart: Mapping meaningful connection and the language of human experience.* Random House.

Bucci, D., Cannon, A., & Ramkarran, A. (2017, September). "Community, Circles and Collaboration: The First 10 Days." https://www.iirp.edu/images/pdf/RsmGIW_Restorative_Approaches-_First_10_Days_1.pdf

Calkins, L. (2001). *The art of teaching reading.* Longman.

CASEL. (2017a). "Examples of social and emotional learning in elementary English language arts instruction." Retrieved from https://casel.s3.us-east-2.amazonaws.com/SEL-in-Elementary-ELA-8-20-17.pdf

CASEL. (2017b). "Sample teaching activities to support core competencies of social and emotional learning." Retrieved from https://casel.s3.us-east-2.amazonaws.com/Sample-Teaching-Activities-to-Support-Core-Competencies.pdf

CASEL. (2020a). "CASEL'S SEL framework: What are the core competence areas and where are they promoted?" Retrieved from https://casel.s3.us-east-2.amazonaws.com/CASEL-SEL-Framework-11.2020.pdf

CASEL. (2020b). CASEL CARES webinar series: SEL as a lever for equity and social justice – Part II: Adult SEL to support antiracist practices. Retrieved from https://casel.org/events/sel-as-a-lever-for-equity-part-two/

Center for Early Childhood Mental Health Consultation. (n.d.). *Ideas for teaching children about emotions.* https://www.ecmhc.org/ideas/emotions.html

Cherng, H. Y. (2016). "Is all classroom conduct equal?: Teacher contact with parents of racial/ethnic minority and immigrant adolescents." *Teachers College Record, 118*(11), 1–32. Retrieved from https://www.tcrecord.org ID Number: 21625.

Children's Community School. (2018). They're not too young to talk about race! Retrieved from http://www.childrenscommunityschool.org/wp-content/uploads/2018/02/theyre-not-too-young-1.pdf

Chugh, D. (2018). *The person you mean to be: How good people fight bias.* HarperCollins.

Clark, K. B., & Clark, M. P. (1947). "Racial identification and preference in negro children." In T. M. Newcomb & E. L. Hartley (Eds.), *Readings in social psychology* (602– 611). Holt, Rinehart & Winston. Retrieved from https://i2.cdn.turner.com/cnn/2010/images/05/13/doll.study.1947.pdf

Cobb, F., & Krownapple, J. (2019). *Belonging through a culture of dignity: The keys to successful equity implementation.* Mimi and Todd Press.

Costello, B., Wachtel, J., & Wachtel, T. (2019). *Restorative circles in schools: A practical guide for educators.* International Institute for Restorative Practices.

DeBeaumont, A., Fairbanks, I., Ahn, J., & Atwood, A. (2021). "If the world was a village of 100 people" *IdeaFest.* https://red.library.usd.edu/idea/291

Delpit, L. D. (2006). *Other people's children: Cultural conflict in the classroom.* W.W. Norton.

Derman-Sparks, L., Edwards, J. O., & Goins, C. M. (2020). *Anti-bias education for young children and ourselves,* 2nd edition. NAEYC

Duyvis, C. [@corinneduyvis]. (2015, September 6). Twitter. #ownvoices, to recommend kidlit about diverse characters written by authors from that same diverse group. https://twitter.com/corinneduyvis/status/640584099208503296

Edmondson, A. (1999). "Psychological safety and learning behavior in work teams." *Adm. Sci. Q.* 44(2):350–83

Edmondson, A. (n.d.). *Building a psychologically safe workplace.* TED Talks. Retrieved from https://www.youtube.com/watch?v=LhoLuui9gX8&ab_channel=TEDxTalks.

Emdin, C. (2017). *For white folks who teach in the hood – and the rest of Y'all too: Reality pedagogy and urban education.* Beacon Press.

Everett, C. C. (2017, November 22). "There is no diverse book." *ImagineLIT.* Retrieved March 28, 2022, from http://www.imaginelit.com/news/2017/11/21/there-is-no-diverse-book

Fountas, I. C., & Pinnell, G. S. (2001). *Guiding readers and writers, grades 3-6: Teaching comprehension, genre, and content literacy.* Heinneman.

Gay. G. (2010). *Culturally responsive teaching: Theory, research, and practice.* Teachers College Press.

Gender Justice in Early Childhood. (2017). "Gender in early childhood V1." [Fact sheet]. Retrieved from www.genderjusticeinearlychildhood.com

Gervais, M. (2018). *Finding mastery podcast 065: Dr. Judson Brewer.* Retrieved April 8, 2019, from https://findingmastery.net/judson-brewer/

Goldberg, G. (2016). *Mindsets & moves: Strategies that help readers take charge, grades 1–8.* Corwin.

Harro, B. (2018). The cycle of socialization. In M. Adams, W. J. Blumenfeld, D. Chase, J. Catalano, K. DeJong, H. W. Hackman, L. E. Hopkins, B. J. Love, M. L. Peters, D. Shlasko, & X Zúñiga (Eds.), *Readings for diversity and social justice.* Routledge.

Harvey, S., & Goudvis, A. (2017). *Strategies that work: Teaching comprehension for understanding, engagement, and building knowledge, grades K–8.* Stenhouse.

Hattie, J. (2018). Visible Learning[Plus]: 250+ influences on student achievement. https://visible-learning.org/wp-content/uploads/2018/03/VLPLUS-252-Influences-Hattie-ranking-DEC-2017.pdf

hooks, bell. (2018). *All about love: New visions.* William Morrow.

Husband, T. (2011). "'I don't see color': Challenging assumptions about discussing race with young children." *Early Childhood Education Journal, 39,* 365–371. https://doi.org/10.1007/s10643-011-0458-9

Jiménez, L. (2021). "Mirrors and windows with texts and readers: Intersectional social justice at work in the classroom." *Language Arts, 98*(3), 156–161.

Kirwan Institute for the Study of Race and Ethnicity. (2018). "Implicit bias module series." Retrieved from http://kirwaninstitute.osu.edu/implicit-bias-training/

Ladson-Billings, G. (2021). "I'm here for the hard re-set: Post pandemic pedagogy to preserve our culture." *Equity & Excellence in Education, 54*(1), 68–78 https://doi.org/10.1080/10665684.2020.1863883

Lawrence-Brown, D., & Sapon-Shevin, M. (2014). *Condition critical: Key principles for equitable and inclusive education.* Teachers College Press.

LeaderFactor. (n.d.). *The complete guide to psychological safety.* Retrieved from https://www.leaderfactor.com/resources/what-is-psychological-safety.

Learning for Justice. (2005). "Speak up! Responding to everyday bigotry." Retrieved from https://www.learningforjustice.org/sites/default/files/2021-05/Speak-Up-2021.pdf

Learning for Justice. (2018). "Social justice standards: The teaching tolerance anti-bias framework." https://www.learningforjustice.org/sites/default/files/2020-09/TT-Social-Justice-Standards-Anti-bias-framework-2020.pdf

Learning for Justice. (2018). "Speak up at school: How to respond to everyday prejudice, bias and stereotypes." Retrieved from https://www.learningforjustice.org/sites/default/files/2019-04/TT-Speak-Up-Guide.pdf

Learning for Justice. (2019). "Let's talk: A guide to facilitating critical conversations with students." Montgomery: The Southern Poverty Law Center. Retrieved from https://www.learningforjustice.org/sites/default/files/2021-11/LFJ-2111-Lets-Talk-November-2021-11172021.pdf

Lieberman. M. (2014). "The social brain and its superpowers." Retrieved from https://www.youtube.com/watch?v=H6L3UMlpn78&ab_channel=BrightSightSpeakers

Madda, M. J. (2019, May 15). "Dena Simmons: Without context, social-emotional learning can backfire." *EdSurge.* https://www.edsurge.com/news/2019-05-15-dena-simmons-without-context-social-emotional-learning-can-backfire

Mar, R. A. & Oatley, K. (2008). The function of fiction is the abstraction and simulation of Social Experience. *Perspectives on Psychological Science, 3*(3), 173–192.

McIntosh, P. (1989). "White privilege: Unpacking the invisible knapsack and some notes for facilitators." Retrieved from https://nationalseedproject.org/Key-SEED-Texts/white-privilege-unpacking-the-invisible-knapsack

Mentor, M., & Sealey-Ruiz, Y. (2021). "Doing the deep work of antiracist pedagogy: Toward self-excavation for equitable classroom teaching." *Language Arts, 99*(1).

Miller, D. (2013). *Reading with meaning: Teaching comprehension in the primary grades.* Stenhouse.

Moore, E., Michael, A., Penick-Parks, M. W., Singleton, G. E., & Hackman, H. (2018). *The guide for white women who teach black boys: Understanding, connecting, respecting.* Corwin.

Mraz, K., & Hertz, C. (2015). *A mindset for learning: Teaching the traits of joyful, independent growth.* Heinemann.

Muhammad, G. (2020). *Cultivating genius: An equity framework for culturally and historically responsive literacy.* Scholastic.

Nathanson, D. L. (1994). *Shame and pride: Affect, sex, and the birth of the self.* W.W. Norton.

Niemi, K. (2020, December 15). "Niemi: CASEL is updating the most widely recognized definition of social-emotional learning. Here's why." *The 74.* https://www.the74million.org/article/niemi-casel-is-updating-the-most-widely-recognized-definition-of-social-emotional-learning-heres-why/

Nieto, S. (1999). *The light in their eyes: Creating multicultural learning communities.* Teachers College Press.

Paris, D., & Alim, H. S. (2017). *Culturally sustaining pedagogies: Teaching and learning for justice in a changing world.* Teacher's College Press.

Pranis, K. (2005). *The little book of circle processes: A new/old approach to peacemaking.* Good Books.

Price-Dennis, D., & Sealey-Ruiz, Y. (2021). *Advancing racial literacies in teacher education: Activism for equity in digital spaces.* Teachers College Press.

Project Implicit. (n.d.). "Implicit association test." Retrieved from https://implicit.harvard.edu/implicit/selectatest.html

Purcell-Gates, V. (2002). "'... As soon as she opened her mouth!': Issues of language, literacy, and power". In L. D. Delpit, & J. K. Dowdy (Eds.), *The skin that we speak: Thoughts on language and culture in the classroom*. New Press.

Riess, H. (2018). *Empathy effect: Seven neuroscience-based keys for transforming the way we live, love, work, and connect across differences*. Sounds True.

Rosenblatt, L. M. (1986). "The aesthetic transaction." *Journal of Aesthetic Education, 20* (4).

Sauer, J. (2014). "Multiple identities, shifting landscapes." In D. Lawrence-Brown & M. Sapon-Shevin, *Condition critical: Key principles for equitable and inclusive education*. Teachers College.

Schulte-Cooper, L. (Fall 2015). "Awards that celebrate diversity in children's literature." *Children and Libraries*. http://dia.ala.org/sites/default/files/resources/awards-diversity.pdf

Sealey-Ruiz, Y. (2021). "The critical literacy of race: Toward racial literacy in urban teacher education." In H. R. Milner IV & K. Lomotey (Eds.), *Handbook of Urban Education, 2nd ed.* Routledge.

Sealey-Ruiz, Y. (n.d.). Archaeology of Self™. Retrieved from https://www.yolandasealeyruiz.com/archaeology-of-self

Serravallo, J. (2010). *Teaching reading in small groups: Differentiated instruction for building strategic, independent readers*. Heinemann.

Serravallo, J. (2015). *The reading strategies book: Your everything guide to developing skilled readers*. Heinemann.

Simmons, D. (2019). "Why we can't afford whitewashed social-emotional learning." *Education Update, 61*(4).

Simmons, D. (2021). "Why SEL alone isn't enough." *Educational Leader, 78*(6).

Stevenson, H. C. (2014). *Promoting racial literacy in schools*. Teachers College Press.

Stevenson, H. C. (2017). *How to resolve racially stressful situations*. TED Talks. Retrieved from https://tedmed.com/talks/show?id=691362.

Tatum, B. D. (2000). The complexity of identity: "Who am I?." In M. Adams, W. J. Blumenfeld, H. W. Hackman, X. Zuniga, & M. L. Peters (Eds.), *Readings for diversity and social justice: An anthology on racism, sexism, anti-semitism, heterosexism, classism and ableism* (pp. 9–14). Routledge.

Tatum, B. D. (2017). "*Why are all the black kids sitting together in the cafeteria?": And other conversations about race*. Basic Books.

Terrell, R. D. & Lindsey, R. B. (2009). *Culturally proficient leadership: The personal journey begins within*. Corwin.

Wachtel, T. (2013). *Dreaming of a new reality: How restorative practices reduce crime and violence, improve relationships and strengthen civil society*. The Piper's Press.

Walther, M. P. (2019). *The ramped-up read aloud: What to notice as you turn the page*. Corwin Literacy.

We Need Diverse Books. https://diversebooks.org

"Wheel of emotions." *Defend Innocence*. https://defendinnocence.org/wp-content/uploads/2019/02/DI_EmotionWheel-v02.pdf

Winfrey, O., & Perry, B. D. (2022). *What happened to you?: Conversations on trauma, resilience, and healing*. Bluebird.

Wiseman, T. (2019). "Theresa Wiseman's four attributes of empathy." Retrieved https://scarlettstrategic.com.au/2019/08/24/theresa-wisemans-four-attributes-of-empathy/

NOTES

NOTES